# How Communication Works

## Creating Win/Win Relationships

---

John K. Pollard, III

ISBN 978-0-942055-38-2

Printed in USA by
Generic Human Studies Publishing
5613 Harco St
Long Beach, CA 90808
USA

# Dedication

*Dedicated to the readers of the future who will learn from this volume long after I'm gone. May you study it carefully and use it wisely.*

# Table of Contents

# Preface

Many people who experience relationship problems have been told they have "a communication problem." What does this mean exactly? Sometimes communication has nothing to do with what is wrong with a relationship. Other times it is the whole problem!

Would you like to know which is which or when is when? Within these pages you will learn a system so clear and simple that you'll be able to easily tell the difference. Get ready for some insights on the communication process you will find nowhere else!

Gathering information from various sources (such as personal discoveries, obscure college texts, life examples, etc.) and combining complex case studies based on the "real world," this volume presents a "best practices" understanding of communication. Once you know How Communication Works, you too will be able to notice and identify any communication problem.

All human interactions require a thoughtful understanding of each of the six steps of communication. This forms the basis for the needs exchange that energizes positive human relationships. Each relationship you are in requires clear and honest messaging for day-to-day function; not to mention when conflicts occur.

It's unlikely that you will just breeze through these pages once or twice and have all your relationship and/or communication problems magically disappear. Because any relationship also involves your many Copartners, it would also be ideal if they too understood these basic principles. Technically this is not required, but it's a big help.

If, from your side only of the seesaw, you practice *conscious* communication you can still have win/win outcomes. You just have to be extra diligent about it. Assuming for the moment that it's just you, prepare to become aware of the deepest levels of exchange that take place between you and your Copartners.

This book is not supposed to put you in a good mood. Its job is to distill the essence of centuries of human discovery investigating relationships. Although this book has knowledge and information available nowhere else, YOU will still need to put what it declares into action to get the results it promises.

# {Ch 1} Introduction

Welcome to the delightful topic of human communication. In an absolutely true sense, nothing is more essential for you to achieve a successful and happy life than knowing and applying *How Communication Works*.

Communication does not take place in a vacuum. It always occurs on a relationship structure. Within these pages you will learn to define and recognize each of the six steps of communication typically buried deep in the details of everyday life.

Cooperating with others in our relationships is the way we meet our various and diverse human needs. When our relationships go well, communication seems to flow, and we are happy. When they are not going so well, communication seems to get in the way, and we become frustrated and unsatisfied.

As individuals over a lifetime we take part in 12 classic relationship categories. These generic structures occur in all cultures as they are essential to fulfill the variety of our many human needs.

Even though relationships are such a common aspect of our everyday lives, we often miss or don't consider some of the deeper dynamics taking place. This book takes you on a gentle yet deep dive into relationship communication.

To learn a complex topic, it's helpful to start by breaking it down into smaller parts. Suppose you want to understand how the body works. You begin by studying the various parts of the body. Once you know the anatomical structures, you study physiology to understand how the brain and organs interact with each other.

In a comparable way, knowing the anatomy of a relationship means first understanding its three basic parts. As a brief review, we know that every relationship must have:

**An Environment**

The Environment is the physical space and location that surrounds the relationship interaction.

**A Seesaw Structure**

This relationship seesaw works exactly like that in a children's playground. Even though this seesaw is a conceptual structure it acts every bit as real as a real seesaw as far as how relationships function in the "real world."

**Two-Copartners**

Sitting on each side of the seesaw, are what we call the Two-Copartners, the participating people on the seesaw of the relationship structure.

Each human relationship has these three structural parts. Yet, the way these parts operate differs slightly in each one. These differences are what distinguishes the 12 major relationships from each other. Once you know and understand how these "anatomical" parts operate within each relationship, you can then understand how the "physiology" of these parts interact.

The idea of separating the anatomy of a relationship from its physiology might be clearer if we use a body part for illustration. Let's say a person begins to have some symptoms that point to their heart. Naturally they would go to their doctor to be evaluated. If the doctor performed tests and discovered the heart was malformed, this would explain the cause of the problem based on anatomy.

If the person's heart was found to be normal in form and structure yet was still presenting symptoms, this means the problem has a functional cause. Even though the heart is anatomically fine, it is not performing as expected for a normal healthy heart.

When a relationship has symptomatic "problems" you start by carefully evaluating its anatomical structure, the Environment, Seesaw, and Two-Copartners. If there is a clear problem with the "anatomy" of these three elements, you have a bigger problem than communication can correct. Even excellent communication does not help a relationship with dysfunctional building blocks.

Even if the "anatomy" of your relationship is judged to be 100% normal, you can still experience "physiology" type problems. Your relationship does have the proper building blocks but is still not working as expected. These are the kind of problems created by faulty communication. Learning the principles and skills of correct messaging from these pages will resolve these types of problems.

Let's say you suitably evaluate your relationship and decide that, yes indeed, all the anatomical parts are present and should be working correctly. In this case the dysfunction is certainly due to communication problems between the Two-Copartners.

This topic of communication has clear principles that apply to all situations. These will be shared and explained thoroughly in the following pages. However, understanding the diversity of dynamics for each relationship is all important for the success of your communication.

For example, the communication interactions within a Parent/Child relationship would be vastly different to those involving a Neighbor/Neighbor relationship. Similarly, the Boyfriend/Girlfriend dynamics would be completely different to those of the Boss/Employee interactions. Each category of relationship has differing needs and themes that revolve around its communication issues.

Just so you know, the book *How Relationships Work* explains the anatomical foundation for each of the 12-Relationships. It describes how and when the three required elements of a relationship are present and healthy as a starting point.

Once you know how relationships are designed to work, then you apply the methods in *How Communication Works* to gain the skills and training necessary to create win/win relationship dynamics. Both books are necessary to fully master the skill of solving any and all would-be relationship problems.

Communication is the exchange of information that takes place on the seesaw structure. Its primary purpose is for you to skillfully dialogue with your Copartners, during which you ask for and exchange the needs which the relationship provides.

Every relationship has the potential for a win/win result. However, the way to ensure this happening is for both Copartners to practice excellent communication on a regular basis. As such, this book presents the foundational basics of human communication. Here you will learn to look for and recognize the aspects of communication that are often missing in unhealthy relationships.

However, this book does not go into detail about the specific needs associated with each of the 12 Generic Relationships. The book serving this purpose is *How Relationships Work* (HRW), the companion volume to this work. The purpose of that book was to explain how each of the 12 main relationships function in exact detail. In a very real sense, this work could have been called, How Relationships Work Volume II.

To begin to evaluate if a relationship has the potential to work correctly, you must be able to assess the three anatomical elements that enable it to function. You must first know *how* relationships are supposed to work before you can apply the purpose for which communication is needed.

The more you gain awareness by reading and understanding these principles, the easier it will be for you to apply "best practice" communication values within your current relationships. Your first step is to apply these principles within your current relationships. Then, if you take the time to evaluate your past relationships, you will see where your problems developed and why those relationships didn't work out.

You are welcome to study communication as a standalone topic. However, the true value of this work is to supplement, complete, and polish the full understanding of relationships. Both books are necessary to receive the complete body of knowledge. Welcome to this exciting and valuable study of human communication.

Once you understand and adopt these simple guidelines, you will know what is normal or abnormal in your relationship world. You will also have the tools to correct any problems you encounter. We are going to begin with a short balloon ride.

# {Ch 2} Relationships Overview: Floating from Above

Imagine floating in a balloon over a city or town. Below you see the multitudes of people involved in various activities. How would you categorize all these many actions taking place below? What is a single idea or concept that could explain all the behaviors of the people as you float above their lives?

Until your balloon lands, you are not near enough to hear what they are saying, or exactly see what they are doing. Yet, you do perceive purposeful activity that appears motivated by something. Faces are not yet distinguishable, although you might be able to tell the gender or age of the people below. There is no direct evidence of governments or politics, yet everyone appears to be striving with a purpose as they live, interact, and go about their daily lives.

## What Is Motivating All These People?

As the balloon descends, we can see that each person is clearly motivated by something. They are moving, talking, driving, and performing all sorts of directed activities but for what purpose? From this overhead view, we can see each person scurrying around doing something. What is that "something" from the big perspective? Whether approaching a big city, a small village, or remote countryside, all the human activity you see revolves around one simple concept.

## Unmet Needs

From the Generic Human Studies (GHS) perspective, we can determine that unmet needs are the fuel that motivates each person that you see. All the activity, all the interactions, and all the driving around occurs because all the various people are seeking to meet one set of needs or another. Every single person is motivated by one or more "unmet needs" they wish to fulfill. So, how do we determine what each person's needs might be?

As humans we have a vast number of potential human needs. There can be so many that at first it can be confusing to try to identify them all. In GHS we use a mental "smart system" to understand and categorize the multitude of needs that people have.

A smart system is a term borrowed from computer programming. It is essentially a menu of set choices guaranteed to be correct because it has been proven and established over so many years. Using a smart system enables you to start from a vague or general area of needs and then mentally drill down to a more specific version of a need.

## Picking the Need

To begin the steps for what we call "picking the need," GHS has grouped the totality of human needs into three areas, Personal, Relational, and Financial. Each grouping of needs is different and excludes all the needs from any other type. It begins by asking yourself the following question, "Is this person's need Personal, Relational, or Financial?"

Determining a need from one of these starting points makes it amazingly easy to dive deeper into the specific need. One of these types of need will always be the correct choice as a starting point. For shorthand this is called the "PRF Needs" smart system. As you become familiar with these three master types of human needs, they will instinctively bring you to a deeper understanding of communication dynamics.

Any time you want to quickly drill down to a specific need, start your focus with one of these three top-level key words: Personal, Relational, or Financial. Once you learn and practice this easy mental trick, you can quickly drill down to the unmet need that you, or another person might have.

Please pay attention to this idea as this is an important mental technique that will pay major dividends for the rest of your life. Each type of need is based on a specific condition. This condition alone determines where to begin searching for the need. Here they are in topic form.

## Personal Needs

Personal needs are assigned and specific to a single person. They are unique to his/her existence and are within his/her own control as well as area of responsibility. When the need involves only one person, it is automatically assigned as a Personal Need.

## Relational Needs

The next group of needs with the PRF mind trick is the Relational category. The number one distinction that separates a Personal from a Relational Need, is as follows. A Relational need requires and involves another person. As soon as another person is required to meet your need, this need becomes Relational.

A Child has needs s/he can only receive from a Parent. A Friend has needs provided by the other Friend. A Boss can only get his/her Boss needs met from an Employee. The only way that you can get a Relational Need met is by being in a relationship with a willing copartner.

## Financial Needs

The final top-level choice to determine a human need is the Financial Needs category. The key aspect here that determines this category is that transaction must involve money. However, the presence of money alone is not the determining factor. Typically, money is the primary driver of the relationship. What does this mean exactly?

When a Parent gives a Child ten dollars for lunch money this is not a Financial Need category. In this situation money is not "the point" of the transaction. The point in this circumstance is that the parent is providing for the child, which is a classic relational need exchanged in the P/C relationship.

However, when the Child uses this money to buy lunch, this becomes a Financial Need. You need money to buy food. The point of this transaction is that you give money and get food. Money is the foundation of the whole transaction. You need to spend money to buy food. And the person selling the food is doing it to make money.

We will further explore each of these three top-level choices in the next chapter. Picking this main category always leads to a next set of three questions. Answering these three questions may also lead to more questions. Taking each step narrows down each need to a specific, well-defined term that cannot be misunderstood. Another nice aspect about the PRF smart system is that once you learn it, you can depend upon its usefulness for the rest of your life.

## Summarizing Needs

So, give these three choices some thought. Can you readily agree and relate to these three main headings? Personal needs connect and pertain to a single person based on his/her desires or preferences. When a second person is needed to fulfill a need, then it's clearly is a Relational Need. And if money is mostly the whole point of the transaction, then it becomes a Financial Need by default. Each of these need areas are mutually exclusive.

In a way, this smart system could also be called common sense. This shows another reason the PRF Needs Smart System is so helpful. It is basic common sense which everyone can agree with since it's obvious. It's this kind of agreement that is essential and fundamental to the success of communication. Without it, communication is impossible. You must be using the same definitions for words with your relationship Copartners when communicating.

In the next chapter we will see how the choice of each top-level need, brings us to the next deeper level of determining the exact need of yourself or your Copartner.

# {Ch 3} Observing Life On "the Street" Level

As our balloon descends to the street level, it's easier to see how human activities are designed to fulfill unmet needs. However, this is still a general observation of motivated activity. We still don't have very many specific details.

Let's say our balloon has now landed. We can now take a stroll "on the street" and watch how people are interacting. Some people are just on their own. Others that we see are engaged in structured activities with other people. It is these activities that take place on various seesaw structures called relationships. Using the PRF Needs smart system, you can now determine more specific application of needs as you drill down to a second level of understanding these three top-level needs.

## Defining PERSONAL Needs (PEM)

Many people at the street level appear to just be doing things by themselves. There doesn't seem to be another person that is part of their activity. They might be eating, or listening to music, or reading a book. They could be exercising, watching TV, or writing in a journal. These activities are random, unique to each person, and appear to be self-motivated. This fits the category of Personal Needs.

Even if you recognize a need as "Personal" it's still not specific enough to be of use in communication. Your next step is to put a Personal Need into one of three sub-categories called Physical, Emotional, or Mental Needs. You do this by asking yourself the follow-up question: Is this person's Personal need Physical, Emotional, or Mental?

All humans have personal needs. Again, this is no major surprise or mystery. Fulfilling personal needs has been part of human history from the dawn of time, and defining these needs is surprisingly easy.

Physical needs have to do with and primarily concern the physical body. Emotional needs have to do with and primarily concern feelings. Mental needs have to do with and primarily concern thinking and mental activity. Each category can then lead to more choices.

Here are some sample needs from each of the three Personal Needs categories:

**Physical Needs:**

- Food
- Shelter
- Safety
- Sleep
- Survival
- Travel

**Emotional Needs:**

- Happiness
- Love
- Caring
- Pleasure
- Joy
- Passion

**Mental Needs**

- Learning
- Discovering
- Teaching
- Knowledge
- Curiosity

Each person that you see who is alone "on the street" has one of these basic PEM needs that primarily motivate his/her behavior. However, the specific intent or purpose for each person's needs depends on his/her individual physical, emotional or mental preferences.

For example, every person needs food to survive, but each person has individual favorites as to what they like to eat. Each person enjoys being entertained but they have a different desired music they like to listen to. Every person has the curiosity to learn, but what topic s/he wants to learn about varies from person to person.

Personal Needs are specific to the individual. Each person alone has his/her own distinctive differences and expressions of the generic personal needs. This is what makes each person unique as an individual.

## Defining Relational Needs (FSW)

We can also see from the street level that there are many people actively engaging with other people. You might see people pushing baby carriages, or engaged in conversation, or even people repairing the street. What these people are doing and why is based on their activities involving the Relational Needs category.

Determining that a need is relational means it must require another person. However, this does not give us enough detail to define the relational need. In the PRF "smart system" the next level to drill down are whether the needs involve Family, Social, or Work (FSW) relationships. We do this by asking the question, "Is this person's need related to Family, Social, or Work activities?"

From this "street level" perspective, we might not be able to know exactly in which category the people we are observing fit, but there are some distinctions. Here are the three main areas.

### Family Relationships

The first groupings we might notice entering the street level are those that seem to have the closest interactions. These are the relationships involving people who are related by blood. Your earliest human awareness began as a helpless infant being taken care of by parents or other caretakers. Being born places you into a family unit, which forms the basic building block of human society. No one single person can exist without a human society. If your parents or other caretakers did not provide for you from birth, you would not have survived to be reading this book.

Parents have children and if your parents have more children, you become a brother or a sister. Your parents had parents, who may or may not have had siblings, who may or may not have had children. Thus, there is a genetic link between each family member.

Depending on your own unique situation, you gradually became aware of other family members within your family unit. Then everyone gets older and new family members arrive.

The needs of Family members are defined by their role in the family. If a Child, you have child needs. If you are a Parent, you have parental needs. If you become a Grandparent, you have grandparent needs. The needs of a Sibling are different to those of the Grandparent. Most people are familiar with this concept of family interactions based on their experience growing up.

Family relationships form the basic core unit of human society. They typically take place in an environment known as the home. Homes are smaller units grouped together into neighborhoods, suburbs, towns, or cities. Wherever they take place, the core Family Relationships structures (and their various permutations) are:

- Parent/Child Relationships
- Sibling/Sibling Relationships
- Grandparent/Grandchild Relationships
- Relative/Relative Relationships
- Adult Child/Aging Parent Relationships

If you enter a home at the street level of your city or town, you will see that the primary and most intimate transactions of society begin with the Family Relationships.

**Social Relationships**

You may also notice "on the street" that not all activity seems to be specifically Family related. There are plenty of people moving around and interacting with others that don't appear to be family members. They seem to be hanging out just talking or running into each other on the street. For the moment we don't see anything like the exchange of money between these participants.

The Social relationships revolve the roles people play with friends, dating partners, neighbors and other non-related members of society. These roles involve relationships that are not part of a biological family, nor do they involve the people where you work. This category includes the additional people who interact with each other in life such as neighbors, fellow students, church members, etc.

As we continue to discover, these are the relationships that occur between people outside of families. These interactions are the Social Relationships. They have the following groupings:

- Friend/Friend Relationships
- Boyfriend/Girlfriend Relationships
- Husband/Wife Relationships
- In-law/In-law Relationships
- Neighbor/Neighbor Relationships

These interactions are the networking glue that binds individual families together with other non-related families within society. Normally there is no blood connection to social relationships nor is money the primary basis for which the relations exist.

As humans we all share the experience of being human. Theoretically, this alone would be enough of a basis to interact or share communication with other humans if we are in the same location.

As the early family tribal groups grew into larger social groupings, they formed cities that eventually became states whereupon countries were established. These wider groups shaped a more distinct culture along with political organizations, a system of laws, and places of worship. As the earlier members of society pass on, they leave a language, culture, and structure of beliefs that continue to live on with their descendants.

**Work Relationships**

And finally, we might notice that indeed there are quite a few human beings involved in what seem to be functionally distinct activities. They could be doing work like driving, picking up the garbage, or repairing the streets.

We also see specific areas where people go to buy food, clothes, and supplies such as bazaars and stores. There are buildings where people store and manage warehouse products. In these locations various people are buying or selling goods, supplying services, or doing such things as advising or teaching.

The relationships in which people group together for the purpose of building things or making money we call Work Relationships. Just to be clear, Work relationships are between people who are working together, for the purpose of creation or commerce.

For example, all the people that work at Company A, are working together. This is as opposed to their clients, customers, or the buyers who go to Company A to buy goods or services. The people who work in a store, are involved in Work Relationships with each other. The customers who shop at this store are not included in this category.

There are two basic types of Work Relationships:

- Boss/Employee Relationships
- Coworker/Coworker Relationships

Whether you are the Boss, Employee, or Coworker you have a set of needs involving your role. These primarily revolve around cooperative work performance and interactions within your work environment. They involve the people you work with to provide or create a service or product.

**Professional Relationships**

There is a fourth relational category called Professional Relationships. As human societies grow and expand, various people within the society specialize in a skill, trade, or endeavor that requires complicated training and/or commitment.

These relationships were created to meet more specialized human needs as society evolved and necessarily involve the exchange of money for services and products. Or they are provided by society itself as a service for its members involving such relationships as:

- Student/Teacher
- Doctor/Patient
- Lawyer/Client
- Police/Citizen
- Politician/Constituent

This fourth category of human relationships is outside the study of communication for our purposes. They follow the same guidelines but vary in many ways between the various human cultures, political, and religious societies. Many professional relationship members have even organized to create a code of conduct, rules, and specialized language to operate within their specialty.

And why would the individual members of society involve themselves in relationships to take part and interact with other members of society—to fulfill their unmet needs of course.

## Defining Financial Needs (EST)

Financial Needs characterize the human activities involved with the earning, spending, and transferring of money. They necessarily involve money and indeed, the flow, transfer, or exchange of money is the primary motivation for the Financial Relationships.

When humans first organized as hunter gatherers, there was no need for money. However, there was a need to trade and exchange goods and services with other communities. Known as the barter system, perhaps one tribal area had a plentiful source of salt, spices, or animal skins. These were valuable items so tribes would exchange what was plentiful in their area for something they desired. These items became a "medium of exchange" because they had a genuine value to other tribes in different locales.

As societies became more agricultural food, cattle, and sheep became early forms of barter. Eventually a neutral and easier way of counting and storing value became important. A more transportable material, such as paper or metal began to be used to keep score and accounts. As societies became agriculturally based these numbers started to accumulate and were passed down to heirs since hunter-gathers were no longer nomadic and land ownership became a concept.

Eventually money became a "thing" because if you had some you could buy other things, and thus it had its own value. Even though you can't eat or drink money, in today's society you can typically purchase all sorts of goods and services. Thus, people began to covet money, even though it has no intrinsic worth on its own.

If stranded on a desert island with no food or water but millions of dollars, you wouldn't live one day longer unless rescued. In which case you would be happy to give all your money to your rescuers for the privilege of another chance at life.

Financial Needs are an interesting type of needs because they intertwine and intermingle with the prior two needs categories. Although not a communication topic per se, all members of a society communicate about money to facilitate the meeting of their Personal (physical, emotional, or mental) needs. For example, we need money to buy food, a music CD, or a ticket to the movies to name three simple examples.

Also, for relationships (family, social, and work) money is needed on a constant basis to function normally. In fact, the work relationships fully revolve around money since most people work for money and their boss or company pays them in salary and wages, etc.

Money itself is a whole subject of conversation since it is so essential for survival in society today. It is also the topic of multiple books, seminars, and indeed entire professions such as accounting or being a financial advisor. If you would like to study a "money book" that provides an authentic system to-manage your money as a person, I recommend, *Your Money or Your Life* (rev. 2008) by Vicki Robin.

In today's world money is part of every aspect of life. Your physical, emotional, mental, family, social and work needs all have financial elements and considerations. How you earn, spend, and transfer money all begin as transactions set up within your family, social, and larger political environments.

Money is super important, but not as important as your Personal and Relational Needs as outlined in this book. Money will not make you happy or satisfy you if your Personal and/or Relational Needs are not fulfilled.

The Financial Needs are listed here briefly to complete the list, but they are not a large part of this book because your Personal and Relational Needs are the ones you must understand to have a "normal" life. However, you will certainly find your upcoming communication skills will come in handy when discussing money and financial topics with others.

**Earning Needs:**

This is where most people in a society must have some form of income or way to earn money to be able to pay for their various PEM and FSW needs. Typically, people meet these needs by their work or professional endeavors.

**Spending Needs:**

Spending needs involve each person's duty to conserve and manage their money to meet his/her PEM and FSW needs. They are answerable to manage their spending of money to purchase the goods or services they deem will to enhance their well-being in some way.

**Transferring Needs:**

Transferring needs revolve around the saving or borrowing of money to supply and sustain your various financial activities.

The category of Financial Needs is an advanced topic. Once you understand the basics of PEM and FSW needs, the EST needs will be easier to manage as they are intertwined with the flows of money needed to fuel the meeting of your basic PEM and FSW needs.

Financial Needs get a mention here to complete the PRF drill-down smart system, but the main pledge of this book is to present the principles of clear communication so that you can define and clarify your Personal and Relational Needs.

Your Personal and Relational Needs categories are soon to be defined on a more meaningful level when we start looking at them from the "Personal Perspective." This begins once our balloon has landed on the street level and we step out of the protected basket we have been riding in. From now on, you are going to be looking at your own needs both for yourself personally, and as one person on your side of a relationship seesaw.

# {Ch 4} Relationships from Your "Personal Perspective"

Let's say the balloon in which we were riding has now landed. We've stepped out of the basket and then magically it disappears. From now on you are on your own in this world. Every move you make from here on takes place from your perspective alone.

This creates your own "Personal Perspective" version of the Personal, Relational, and Financial need types which you must strive to fulfill. Your means of doing this will be communication. As of now this whole theoretical situation of "unmet needs" has become real. This conversation is now about you meeting your own Personal and Relational needs.

It's important to highlight that your Personal Needs are yours and yours alone. You are responsible to know what they are and to meet them as best you see fit. It's unlikely anyone else will care about your Personal Needs, because they have their own to worry about.

It's also applies that another person's Personal Needs are his/hers alone and specific to *their* body, emotions, and mind. Part of positive communication is to allow everyone the right, responsibility, and ownership for their own Personal Needs.

For the moment, let's discuss you and you alone. It turns out you now have a wide variety of Personal Needs that are Physical, Emotional, or Mental in nature. Bottom line, you need to meet these needs for yourself as no one else has been properly assigned to this task.

Of course, you are aware of many of these needs. Depending on your age, background, education, life experience and many more factors, you have already done your best to meet these needs as you became aware of them. So how does your mission to meet your own needs fit into the Generic Human Studies paradigm?

We already know that needs are supplied from within relationships. To fulfil personal needs in GHS we present a concept called SELF-Parenting. This is the idea that your mind, as your Inner Parent, is parenting your emotions, as the Inner Child, in exactly the same way that you were parented by your outer parents.

Since this concept has been taught since 1986, hopefully you've heard about it, read the book, practiced the daily sessions, and are part of the website. If not, you are welcome to check out www.selfparenting.com at your leisure.

It turns out that you were taught how to think and act by your parents. Yet your emotions are the same within you now as they were when you were a child, even if now you are an adult. You may not have considered this before, but your thoughts and your emotions are definitely two separate parts of your mind in the way that they communicate with each other.

If you had a positive family upbringing and experience, then you will have been taught and absorbed a positive SELF-Parenting style. If you had a negative or abusive family upbringing, then your SELF-Parenting style will be negative and abusive. As a "normal" part of growing up in this world you were trained as an adult to parent your "Inner Child" in the same way your outer parents parented you.

*SELF-Parenting the Complete Guide to Your Inner Conversations* explains this foundational idea of how your mind works. The ideal role of your Inner Parent is to love, support, and nurture your Inner Child on a consistent daily basis.

You were born and live within a human body. The mind that runs your body has ongoing "inner conversations" that take place the whole time you are awake. Many explanations have been hypothesized for the mind and how it works. Whatever way that you believe the mind works, you strive to meet your PEM needs using your mind to the best of your ability.

When SELF-Parenting you learn how to meet your PEM needs as the Inner Parent by openly and directly listening and responding appropriately to the needs of your Inner Child.

Based on your Inner Conversations, your mind and emotions communicate with each other on an ongoing basis. This is how you make your various decisions as you go through your days, weeks, months, years, decades, and life. Every decision you make is a SELF-Parenting decision.

All the aspects of communication that you will learn in this book also apply to your Inner Conversations. However, your Inner Conversations are deep inside your mind. It takes special methods to learn how to recognize these two voices, teach them how to communicate, and interact with each other in a positive way.

If this area is of interest for you, you can study the SELF-Parenting materials and learn the various ways to use these methods to meet your personal needs. It's also possible you may have zero problems meeting your personal physical, emotional, or mental needs. It all depends how you were parented growing up.

## Moving On to "Outer" Relationships

Most people want to understand communication to improve one or more outer relationships. Next we are going beyond the anatomical parts of a relationship into the flow of information being passed back and forth by the relationship Copartners.

We are going to follow as you enter and exit a variety of relationship structures described in the prior chapters for the purpose of meeting your various Relational (FSW) needs. Here is where the understanding of outer communication becomes vital. Once you become involved on specific relationship seesaws, you require skillful communication to share and exchange with your Co-partners for the purpose of meeting your FSW needs.

Over time human societies developed ways to make things easier so that each generation would not have to start over from nothing. Each of the 12 Generic Relationships meets a specific aspect of human needs that no other relationship meets. It turns out that by far your first relationship is your most important.

You began your life being born into a Parent/Child relationship. Without this relationship you would not be alive. Think about this for a moment. Do you think you might have understood this on a deeper level as a child? Your day to day existence revolved around your parents as caretakers.

From your parents you were also exposed to a wide range of relationships they were already dealing with. For example, your parents had parents. They may have had brothers and sisters. They had neighbors; they socialized, worked, worshipped, and entertained themselves among larger groups of people. You grew up within all this indoctrination and didn't even realize it at the time.

Beneath your conscious awareness you were gently yet inevitably socialized into specific customs and various relationships based on the cultural and political systems where you lived. Because you lived in a sea of relationships, there was communication all around you.

By growing up and observing others, you automatically began to seek your primary needs by copying what they did around you. Some of these methods were successful, others not so much.

What happened during this ongoing process is that we internalized the communication styles of our parents and peers. To practice and develop our own interaction skills, we copied what we saw around us. Because learning our language was so "normal," we never really learned specific details about communication.

Since we've been immersed in communication from the day we were born, it just seems to be a natural part of life like the air we breathe. This idea has been compared to that of being like a fish born in water. If a fish has always been swimming around in water, it's not going to even think about water.

The trouble being that when communication problems begin to appear not everyone knows what's going on. In fact, as a person growing up you may have learned styles of communication that were extremely negative. Through dysfunctional family dynamics you could have been taught ways to attempt meeting your needs that were unbelievably bad.

As a child and family member, whatever styles of communication you learned growing up will seem "normal" because you didn't know any other alternatives. But as you mature and branch out into the wider world, you might find that other families and cultures communicate differently from what you experience as familiar. This can lead to various levels of success or failure as you go about in the "real world" trying to meet your unmet needs.

When you start having problems in your 12-relationship types, you might not realize that these issues are caused by how you were previously and mostly unconsciously taught to communicate.

Given the sheer volume and complexity of human relationships you may not understand the many ways that relationships can fail or be successful. As you move further away from your family of origin you might find that the communication styles used in your family may not work so successfully in the "real world."

Given society's general lack of understanding as to how relationships work in the first place, it's extremely likely that lack of clear communication is at the core of every true relationship problem. If so, neither Copartner in the relationship may understand what the issues are because each learned his/her own version of how communication works within their own family. Thank goodness for this book!

# {Ch 5} Now Our Study of Communication Begins

It's a condition for reading this book that you understand the basics of how relationships work. I trust you've reviewed the book of that name and understand the key anatomy that must be present for a relationship to have a chance of success. Once the three relationship elements are in place, both copartners have the status, the opportunity, and the obligation to practice positive communication skills to make their relationship successful.

When you don't know how relationships work, communication doesn't help much anyway. You could be communicating perfectly in a bad relationship, only it won't help you at all. This is why you must have a solid understanding of the Environment, the Seesaw Structures, and the 2-Copartner elements for each of the 12 major relationships.

Now that you are "on the ground" you want to do everything possible so that at least your personal relationships, the ones in which you are a Copartner, have a chance for a win/win outcome.

Let's start by asking some basic questions such as:

- How and when do relationships begin? (We already know why!)
- How long do relationships continue?
- When do relationships end?
- How do we know when a relationship is positive or negative? (i.e. meeting the needs of its individual participants).
- How can we evaluate the success or failure of a relationship?

These considerations are most important for win/win relationships. It's not enough to know that people enter relationships to fulfill unmet needs. There is more to it.

Just entering a new relationship is no guarantee that your needs will be met. In fact, you can even have bad things happen if you are not careful. Things you didn't know you even had can be taken away.

Consider that you are now in a unique and personal relationship, with a specific person. Both of you ideally want the relationship to be a win/win experience. You are on one side of the relationship seesaw with your Copartner on the other. You know the name the name of the relationship, which stipulates the Roles and the Rules by which to play. Here is when and where communication enters the picture.

## When Do Relationships Begin?

Relationships begin when two people start communicating on a specific relationship structure; not before, not after, but when. It doesn't have to be "in person". It can be by letter or on the phone or through advertising, but once two people begin to communicate interactively, their relationship begins.

In Generic Human Studies we designate this relationship as "personal." This defines the relationship as between just two people together on the seesaw. Only these participants have any real say about this exact relationship. Add to this perspective that you are one of the two people involved on each seesaw.

You know the three main relationship groupings: Family, Social, and Work. It would be simple to determine the number of personal relationships you have and put each into its own section. Once your Copartners have taken their respective sides on the relationship seesaw with you, your relationship begins.

This is called an "instance" in computer programming which is when the hypothetical ________/________ relationship becomes an actual relationship. Now there is a genuine Environment, a bonified Seesaw Structure, with a Copartner seated on either side. This produces a "real world" example of what was a theoretical model. The GHS model is no longer a theory, once two people create a new instance of a relationship in the "real world."

Each relationship is designed to provide a precise collection of needs. Both Copartners are meant to meet the needs of the other. Communication is the means by which a Copartner gives and gets his/her unmet needs met. Let's establish some additional ground rules in regard to communication.

## How Long Do Relationships Continue?

Relationships continue as long as the Two-Copartners continue to communicate. How long will their relationship last? It will last as long as the Two-Copartners continue to spend time and energy communicating.

## When Do Relationships End?

Relationships end when the two people in the relationship stop communicating. As long as the Two-Copartners are on the seesaw, they are in a relationship. Until communication ends, the relationship is still active. When they stop communicating, the relationship is over.

What have we learned so far about communication and relationships?

- Relationships start when communication begins.
- Relationships end when communication stops.

From this information we can extract that that excellent communication is the key for all the relationship activities in between.

## How Do We Know If A Relationship Is Positive or Negative?

We can see that relationships are taking place because people are communicating on the relationship seesaw. When they start communicating the relationship starts. When they stop communicating the relationship stops.

With all these multitude of relationships we are viewing, how do we know if they are successful, or failing, or what? Since so many people are attempting to meet their needs in relationships, is there some way we can tell if the relationship is working? Yes, there is!

## The Four Possible States of a Relationship

The answer is that every relationship exists in one of four potential states or conditions. Each state is based on how each Copartner is getting her/his needs met.

There are Two-Copartners on a seesaw and each one can either be winning or losing. Thus, the four possible categories of any relationship are:

- Lose/Lose
- Win/Lose
- Lose/Win
- Win/Win

Each person on a relationship seesaw is either in a state of winning or losing. There is no 50/50 or half winning/half losing for a person on his/her side.

This condition does not remain static or permanent. It can switch back and forth depending on the situation. But it does have to be explicitly defined. Each Copartner decides based on his/her own opinion and point of view whether or not they are winning or losing.

**Lose/Lose**

The Lose/Lose relationship is when neither Copartner in the relationship is getting her/his needs met.

- Both Parent and Child are losing.
- Both Husband and Wife are losing.
- Both Boss and Employee are losing.

**Win/Lose**

The Win/Lose situation is where one of the Copartners is getting his needs met.

- The Brother is winning, and the Sister is losing.
- The Boyfriend is winning, and Girlfriend is losing.
- Coworker A is winning, and Coworker B is losing.

**Lose/Win**

This situation, using the above example, is when the Copartner on the other side of the seesaw is winning.

- The Brother is losing, and Sister is winning.
- The Boyfriend is losing, and the Girlfriend is winning.
- Coworker A is losing, and Coworker B is winning.

Some examples from other relationship seesaws would be:

- The Grandparent is losing, and the Grandchild is winning.
- Friend A is losing, and Friend B is winning.
- The Boss is losing, and the Employee is winning

Each perspective in the above naturally depends on which role you are playing, and whether you feel you are winning or losing on your side of the seesaw.

**Win/Win**

Clearly, the ideal situation for each of the 12-Generic Relationships is when both Copartners on the relationship seesaw are getting their needs met.

- The Aging Parent is winning, and the Adult Child is winning.
- Neighbor A is winning, and Neighbor B is winning.
- The Boss is winning, and the Employee is winning.

So, let's ask ourselves the next question.

## How Do We Know When A Relationship Is Successful or Failing?

Next comes an important piece of the relationship puzzle, so pay attention. You may never see this information in any other book. And you may not even believe it until life teaches you so.

A relationship is ONLY successful:

WHEN

- You are getting your relationship needs met on your side of the seesaw.

AND

- Your Copartner is getting his/her relationship needs met on his/her side of the relationship seesaw.

Next is also an important understanding which is not always apparent, but you need to know this deeply if you wish to have an abundance of win/win relationships in your life. This is not always evident, especially if you are on the winning side in a relationship.

A relationship is ALWAY failing:

WHEN

- You are not getting your relationship needs met in the relationship.

OR

- Your Copartner is not getting his/her relationship needs met, even if you are.

## Why Are You Losing in A Relationship Even If Your Needs Are Being Met? (If Your Copartner Is Losing)

Understand this key principle from this moment on. Relationships are dysfunctional unless both Copartners are meeting the needs that the relationship is intended to provide. This includes you getting your needs met as well as your Copartner on the other side of your seesaw.

Clearly if both Copartners are losing in a relationship this is bad. You will certainly find your relationship distasteful if you are losing and the other person is winning. And, as your relationship understanding grows, you will also learn to be unhappy even if you are winning and the other person is losing. How could this be?

This may seem strange at first. Why should it bother you when you are getting your needs met, even if your Copartner is not? To grasp the answer to this question and put its principles into action in your life will create a turning point in your relationship understanding.

Perhaps a person who is "winning" in a relationship will find it nearly impossible to "feel" this is bad when they are feeling so good. Maybe it's "human nature" not to look too closely at the other person's side of the seesaw when things are going your way. However please consider this concept carefully from the long-term perspective.

Meeting your own needs at the expense of another is conspicuous consumption. It's similar to the concept that "there is no free lunch." If, the normal exchange of needs in a relationship is not being met for your Copartner, (whichever type of relationship you are in) you are essentially getting something for nothing.

When you feel good or happy, it doesn't feel like something for nothing. In fact, it can feel great! Your winning may feel good in the short term; however, this "feeling good" is really burning karma for you in the same way that burning down centuries of rain forest allows you to graze cows for a year or two.

If your Copartner says in effect, "I'll meet your needs even though you don't meet mine" then being in a relationship with this person will eventually demand karmic payback. You can cruise along milking the honey if you wish. However, if you make any plans based on this relationship, it will be a mistake.

Eventually, the relationship must fail if the other person is not getting his/her relationship needs met, at which time your needs will no longer be met. You will not always be in a position to see or predict the way you are going to wind up losing but lose you will.

Here is one way you can lose by getting your needs met "for free" in a relationship. Because you are getting some needs met "for free" this means that you have extra resources available. This allows you the "opportunity" to "invest" in other relationships where you will lose.

You may find this idea to be debatable. Not everyone new to this idea may fully understand how this works without some "real world" experience. Just know that from the perspective of HRW, a relationship is negative, unless it is functioning as a Win/Win relationship. You are losing in any relationship where your Copartner is not getting his/her needs met, even if (especially if) your needs are met.

Why is this exactly? Obviously if both people are losing the relationship is negative. But why if one is winning and the other losing is that negative? Why can't at least one person be happy, especially if it's you!

When either person is losing, the relationship is not functioning properly. The energy flow required by the relationship (meeting unmet needs) is only flowing one way on the seesaw and is not being replenished/recycled. The seesaw has enough energy to continue moving but is dysfunctional at its core and thus negative.

The person who is winning may think everything is okay and that s/he is in a great relationship, but eventually something is going to happen. It's a law of nature. Either the relationship will go sour, or the person who is winning at the expense of the other losing gets overconfident and makes fatal mistakes in this or another relationship.

Think of it this way. Let's say you borrowed a large sum of money long ago, which you never paid back. And now, you've just earned that same amount. Ideally you would use the new money to pay back what you owe. But then it will "feel" like you lost it as you will have nothing again.

If you spend the money on some shiny new "something" this will feel like a positive even though you logically understand that the money you are spending is owed to someone else. Even if you earned this "new" money all by itself you still know that you owe the money you borrowed. Or maybe you conveniently forget this for the time being.

This doesn't even address why someone would continue to be in a relationship where s/he was not winning. This is often a lack of self-esteem on the part of the person. Maybe they feel that being used and abused has some upside. They may be repeating a family dynamic that they witnessed as children. There could be many potential reasons because it happens a lot. Whatever the reason, it's a negative strategy for all concerned.

If you seem to be getting a free ride in a relationship even though it feels great, you are incurring a debt that you will have to repay, or it will be extracted from you by another relationship. You are just spending freely of gifts you have been given and there is no free lunch.

Unfortunately, in an intimate personal relationship it is not always easy to realize you are "borrowing" this energy you didn't earn. Because you are getting your needs met you feel good about this. It's human nature to possibly justify that everything is okay. If you can recognize this situation and do something to change it, you can prevent the eventual consequence of a failed relationship.

Most typically, this is a SELF-Parenting flaw for the individual who would allow him/herself to do this to someone, as well as for the person who is willing to be on the losing end of such a relationship seesaw.

# {Ch 6} Communicating In Personal Relationships

We have established that a Personal Relationship refers to one in which you are involved personally, as opposed to the same category of relationship in which you are not involved. It just helps to differentiate between the two concepts. Being personally involved in a relationship is vastly different from knowing or hearing about a non-personal relationship or seeing one on TV or in a movie.

This becomes of greater importance after observing "from above" that all people are motivated in relationships by unmet needs and then noticing "on the street" that entering relationships is how people strive to meet their needs. It turns out that you, the reader, are also human. You have unmet needs and you also need outer relationships to meet them like everyone else.

Consequently, you are compelled to enter real and specific relationship structures. From there on its personal; this is about you and your life. On this level you can't see and don't care about anyone else's relationships.

This are *your* family relationships, *your* social situations, and *your* work problems.

What you can see or care about on this level deals with the specific relationships you are in. Here is when you need to know more about specific details such as:

- What kind of person should I look for to be in a relationship?
- What relationship seesaw am I on anyway?
- How can I get *my* needs met in this relationship?
- What specific needs am I trying to meet?
- What state is *my* relationship in?
- If something is wrong with this relationship, is it me or my Copartner's fault?
- Am I in the proper relationship structure for meeting my needs?
- What rules, techniques, or methods can I use with this person to enhance the meeting of my needs in this specific relationship?

This is where the action starts with communication. Communication is the method and means to successfully navigate relationship issues. It also forms the core basis to answer each of the above questions.

Since this is a book about communication and not relationships per se, we are now going to take a deep dive into the essential heart of communication to see what these parts are and how they work. From there we can start using this knowledge within our personal relationships to get our needs met.

## Some Communication Terms

Stay alert as you explore this chapter. Some of what I'm writing about you may or may not have already known. And you may or may not have been exposed to other bits and pieces. Mixed in with this will be information you have never heard.

I feel this is important to say because you will be taught some answers to questions even the experts don't have. This is because Generic Human Studies provides a system, a basis for you to KNOW what you know.

Communication is not a new topic. There have been centuries of books and studies written about communication. It's not like people and scholars don't know this topic is important. It is a subject taught in every high school and college.

Generic Human Studies has dug deeply into this subject matter to establish a unique perspective and point of view to describe how communication works. To present this knowledge clearly it was necessary to create specific terminology and style by which it is taught. This is the beauty and strength of GHS. Here you can easily learn and understand the hidden dynamics of communication that even most experts don't know. Read on.

### What Is Communication?

First let's ask this question, "What is communication?" As a starting point, we can define the purpose of communication as a two-way exchange of information between

Two-Copartners. Although this is simple, easy, and perhaps the classic definition, it's not quite the whole story.

**What Is the Purpose of Communication?**

Learn this now, lock it in your memory forever. What is the purpose of communication? Why are we investing so much time and energy communicating all the time? Why? Why? Why? What is the purpose behind our communication? What is our goal?

Answer — to meet our unmet needs.

You, I, all of us communicate to meet our unmet needs. We have something physical, emotional, mental, or relational that we want, and communication is the way we go after it. Relationships are about meeting our unmet needs. Therefore, the primary method to get your needs truly met, is to communicate your unmet needs to your Copartner while being on the correct relationship seesaw.

Clearly, we need to be in the appropriate relationship structure that provides the needs we are after. This is where the book, *How Relationships Work* comes in. By defining each of the 12-Human Relationships we know what needs they are designed to provide when working correctly. Once we are in the right relationship with the proper Environment, Structure, and Two-Copartners, it's communication that energizes the needs exchanged back and forth on the seesaw.

We can now further define communication as a two-way exchange of information between Two-Copartners on the appropriate seesaw, for the purpose of meeting their unmet needs.

## Defining More Terms

To probe deeper into understanding this intricate process called communication, we are going to define several more terms. Each of these words sum up a single aspect of interaction that most people never think about. Here is where you are learning deeper aspects of communication that aren't easy to find.

Knowing these terms and how to use them properly will give you a superb understanding of the communication process. There is nothing complicated about these terms or concepts. But until you've heard them explained in the GHS way, this combination of factors may never have occurred to you.

Since relationship problems are often blamed on a "failure to communicate," let's look even deeper at a communication exchange to see where this breakdown is likely to occur.

## The "Sender" And The "Receiver"

Two terms that will be easy to grasp are the "Sender" and the "Receiver."

### The Sender:

The Sender is the person sending his/her personal thoughts and feelings to another person with a desire to express an unmet need.

**The Receiver:**

The Receiver is the person who is intended to receive the personal thoughts and feelings the Sender wants to express. Within any relationship either Copartner could be the Sender or Receiver at any stage. Both sides of the seesaw are equal, so the Two-Copartners alternate these roles back and forth all the time.

The best way to begin understanding this "2-way" process is to study one half as a "single" communication. In this case there is one Sender and one Receiver. A single message describing an unmet need is sent by the Sender to be received by the Receiver.

**Unmet Needs As "Personal Thoughts and Feelings"**

We know from the "observation" and "street level" views of relationships that we all have unmet needs. Unfortunately, as individuals we don't often go around thinking to ourselves consciously, "I have unmet needs, I have unmet needs, I have unmet needs."

What we do instead is have what GHS calls "Personal Thoughts and Feelings." These take place naturally as inner conversations inside our mind between our mental thoughts and our emotional heart.

It is our unmet needs, concealed within our personal thoughts and feelings that drive our behavior. Whenever we think or feel that we are missing something in our life, we become motivated to seek out and meet this need.

Depending on the situation each person has his/her own mixture of thoughts and feelings of which they are variously conscious or unconscious. Most people are not typically aware that they have unmet needs, they simply sense the thoughts and feelings that motivate their behavior.

Understand that a person's thoughts and feelings are the drivers of communication. It is the Sender's thoughts and feelings that stimulate him/her to seek to meet their needs.

Now we can see a single communication as the Sender's one-way expression of thoughts and feelings to the Receiver. As mentioned, these roles can reverse at any time but for right now, we are describing the Sender sending thoughts and feelings to a Receiver.

However, before we continue there is a crucial component, a big trouble spot, between any Sender and Receiver.

### What Is the Biggest Barrier to Communication?

Here comes a big one. The greatest obstacle between Two-Copartners trying to communicate their thoughts and feelings in a relationship is something GHS calls "the GAP."

The quirkiest part about this "barrier," is that technically it is not even a thing; it is in fact empty space. But it might as well be as wide as the Grand Canyon when things are not going right.

## Defining "The GAP"

The GAP is the physical distance, the empty space between the Sender who desires to communicate with the Receiver. The GAP is what separates one person's private, personal world from the other person. The GAP is what is between you, me, and everyone else, and yet you could read 100 books on communication and never see it mentioned.

Even though it is only empty space, the GAP is the biggest hurdle to know about and overcome when communicating. Until you can send what you personally think and feel across the GAP, you will never be successful with relationships. Understanding how communication works is to learn about and deal appropriately with "the GAP."

## How and Why Does the Barrier of The GAP Make Communication So Difficult?

Until you are introduced to the concept of the GAP, you might never recognize how powerful a part it plays in preventing your personal thoughts and feelings from being received by another person, even if they are very close to you.

Here is the problem. What you want to communicate (your unmet needs in the form of your personal thoughts and feelings) cannot readily be sent across the GAP. Your thoughts and feelings are in your mind and heart. There is no practical way to hook a wire from your brain to another person's brain to directly transfer your thoughts and feelings to that person. If you could, you would be crossing the GAP using the wire.

To understand the concept of the GAP more fully, try this experiment. Have a friend stand next to you. Generate some thoughts and feelings inside your mind. Without saying or doing anything ask your friend to tell you what you are thinking and feeling while you sit there like a stone.

What do you think will happen? If you don't say or do anything, even your best friend can't know what you are thinking and feeling! The reason is that your thoughts and feelings take place inside your body between your heart and mind.

A person outside your body can't see or hear what you are thinking or feeling. It's this invisible barrier we call the GAP, that prevents your friend from having a clue as to what your actual thoughts and/or feelings truly are.

## How Does A Person Communicate Across the Gap?

To cross this barrier called the GAP requires something physical to act as a transfer device. Keep this key point in mind. Since everyone is unconsciously involved in communicating every day, we never stop to consider the physical methods we use to make this transfer. Yet, it is a fact that without some physical method or device for crossing the GAP, we could never accurately communicate our personal thoughts and feelings to anyone.

To transfer our thoughts and feelings to others, we humans use a physical transfer device, what in Generic Human Studies is called Observable Behavior.

## What Is Observable Behavior? (OB)

Observable Behavior (OB) is what a person says and/or does.

### What A Person Says

What a person says includes all the sounds s/he could make such as normal speech, whispering, screaming, moaning, or any sound from a sigh to a snore.

### What A Person Does

What a person does includes the full range of potential physical actions such as facial gestures and expressions, smiling, rolling your eyes, body positions, waving the arms, clasping the hands, typing, writing, sign language, waving a flag, or any other physical actions. This also includes sitting still like a statue and doing nothing.

What a person says or does is something that can be seen and observed by others. This is why we call it OB, or Observable Behavior.

## What Is an Outer Metaphor to Clarify Observable Behavior (OB)?

Sometimes it helps to have an outside metaphor to understand this concept. Therefore, we say that, Observable Behavior is best represented by what a video camcorder (camera with microphone) would record if it were filming a person during the act of communicating. This camcorder would pick up all the sounds a person makes (what they say) as well as any actions or body movements (what they do) such as hand gestures, body positions, and eye contact.

Also note within this definition of Observable Behavior, that this same camcorder could never record the person's thoughts or feelings since they cannot be seen or heard, and thus could not be recorded.

## What Separates Thoughts & Feelings from Observable Behavior as Far as The GAP Is Concerned?

As you may already have figured out, a person's thoughts and feelings are within the private domain of his/her mind and heart. Observable Behavior is the public representation of what a person says or does.

The key difference between the two is that it is impossible for a person's thoughts and feelings to cross the GAP. To receive communication (shared thoughts and feelings) from the other side of the GAP, the Receiver MUST be able to see or hear something from their side.

For example, you can read or hear what I am saying in this book. That is because it has been written down or spoken as something that can be seen or heard. But you can't hear what I'm thinking and feeling, because this can't be recorded. Here, I'll prove it to you. I'm thinking and feeling something right now, (pause), what is it?

The only way you can even begin to interpret what I am thinking and feeling, is for me to say or do something you can hear or see.

## More About Observable Behavior (OB)

Let's dive a bit deeper into this concept of Observable Behavior. No true disagreement should exist when discussing what happens as Observable Behavior. A person either combed his hair or he didn't. She went swimming, running, or both. He climbed the stairs, fell down the stairs, or destroyed the stairs with an axe. She said these exact words, in a loud voice, a whisper, or a scream. A dog barked; a taxi hit that pole. Whatever a video camera would visually and audibly record is observable behavior.

On the other hand, if a video camera was not present to record some Observable Behavior, there could easily be a conflicting version of events as witnessed by others. If ten different people watched the same event, there could be ten different versions of what happened, according to the eyewitnesses. However, if ten people were watching a videotape of the event, all ten people would ideally be able to agree what is, or is not OB, based on what is seen and heard on the video recording.

## What Is the Bottom Line?

To communicate effectively back and forth in relationships, Copartners must use Observable Behavior. People watch and listen to each other's Observable Behavior (what they say and do) with the goal of interpreting the personal thoughts and feelings of the Sender.

Let us take our next listen at the GHS definition of communication and see how it sounds now, with this new insight.

In GHS, we define Communication as the act of expressing your personal thoughts and feelings (unmet needs) using Observable Behavior across the GAP to another person.

We have a Sender, with personal thoughts and feelings (unmet needs), who wishes to communicate them across the invisible and mostly unrecognized barrier of the GAP, to a listener (the Receiver), who must be able to see or hear something for this communication to take place.

Next let's look even deeper into the role of the Sender in communication.

# {Ch 7} Who Is the Sender: A Deeper Look

## Who Is the Sender?

The Sender is the person or Copartner with an unmet need. S/he is the person sending a message for this need to be met. What kind of need could it be? To "drill down" to the next level, we look to see if their need is primarily Personal or Relational. These choices are:

**Personal Needs**

- Physical
- Emotional
- Mental

**Relational Needs**

- Family
- Social
- Work
- (Professional)

To review, **Personal Needs** apply specifically to the individual in an "inner" relationship. The communication here takes place between their Inner Parent and Inner Child as described in *SELF-Parenting: The Complete Guide to Your Inner Conversations.*

However, these same PEM need categories also appear within **Relational Needs** in outer relationships because physical, emotional, and mental needs are provided by each role in the 12 Relationship Structures. For example, a parent has physical, emotional, and mental needs, as do a Friend, or an Employee, etc. See *How Relationships Work* for specific details.

## Let Us Further Ask; "What Are The Steps of Being A Sender?"

The simple role of the Sender is to communicate his/her need. However, what does a Sender actually DO to communicate his/her need across the GAP? To begin to clearly communicate, a Sender must ideally take three precise steps:

Step 1. The Sender recognizes with clarity that they have an unmet need as represented by their thoughts and feelings.

Step 2. The Sender then translates (also called "encoding") their need (based on thoughts and feelings) into Observable Behavior that represents their need.

Step 3. The Sender sends her/his OB (words and/or deeds) across the GAP.

If the Sender can do this, from their half (on their side of the Gap), the communication attempt is complete from their perspective. What do we know about these steps so far?

## Step 1: The Sender Must Know His/Her Unmet Need

For the Sender to know what need s/he is thinking or feeling about is much more of a problem then you might think. Why? Because to accurately recognize what your need is, you must be listening to and paying close attention to your Inner Conversations.

Having spent decades with the SELF-Parenting Program deeply exploring what people are thinking and feeling, I can tell you that the majority of people who don't practice daily SELF-Parenting sessions are only vaguely aware of the most superficial aspects of their Inner Conversations.

If you are reading this book and have been practicing SELF-Parenting for a year or more, how many people do you know that are truly listening to and in touch with their Inner Conversations, their exact thoughts and feelings?

If you are practicing the SELF-Parenting Program, how many times were you unclear about what you were thinking and feeling until you wrote it down in your sessions? Sometimes it takes a person several days, possibly weeks, to fully understand and interpret one's own Inner Conversations; myself included.

Becoming consciously aware of your Inner Conversations is the personal foundation for you to understand your unmet needs, communication, and relationships. Without conscious SELF-Parenting, you are like a blind person stumbling in the dark. If you have practiced SELF-Parenting and then stopped, or have never experienced the SELF-Parenting Program, now is a good time for you to make a commitment to this magnificent method for understanding the deepest levels of your Inner Conversations.

Not knowing one's needs as expressed within her/his inner conversations creates a major problem. If the Sender is not fully aware of what s/he is thinking and feeling (their 2-sided Inner Conversations) how can this person, put his/her thoughts and feelings into mindful Observable Behavior? The most you can expect is this person might have a vague idea of something they would like/want or an uncomfortable feeling of something they do not like/want.

Therefore, the first information a Sender needs is to have a clear and precise idea of what s/he is thinking and feeling. This is the water that fills the communication well. The first obstacle that occurs in communication is that the Sender does not even know what specific type or category of a need s/he is hoping to have met.

This can occur for many reasons. During a relationship crisis, there might be a flood of thoughts and feelings. You could have hundreds of thoughts and feelings in a minute, which would take an hour to write out, much less examine and/or interpret. This is one aspect of the problem.

Another is that possibly one voice, typically the Inner Parent or sometimes the Inner Child, is the loudest voice in the Inner Conversations. Thus, the other voice is not even being heard or acknowledged. This means that one side of your inner conversations may be selfishly demanding something the other side doesn't even want or care about.

You could also have conflicting needs between the Inner Parent and Inner Child. Perhaps the Inner Parent has one agenda and the Inner Child has another. One voice might be more dominating; the other more withdrawn. Maybe one voice has more altruistic goals than the other? Much of the time whichever side is the loudest is the one that "wins." Who knows which is which?

## Step Two: The Sender Must Make His/Her Unmet Need Third-Party Verifiable by Accurately Translating Thoughts and Feelings into Observable Behavior

Just because you, the Sender, may be aware of YOUR thoughts and feelings doesn't mean that you are necessarily able to communicate them. Let's say that you, as the Sender, are fully in touch with your need. You know exactly what you want inside your Inner Conversations.

To begin communicating for this need to be met, what must happen? (Pause) You have to translate your thoughts and feelings into Observable Behavior. Without a conscious understanding along with some practice, this is not as easy as it might sound.

Let's say that you like someone a lot, and you want him or her to know. The simplest way to translate this need into observable behavior is to say something like, "Hey, I like you a lot and I want to get to know you better." You could say this on the phone, send them a letter, or tell them in person, as a clear means of sending your message "across the GAP."

But how easy is this for the average person who doesn't really want to be rejected? Moreover, why is it so easy for me to say and do in this book, but so hard to do if I were in this situation myself?

Therefore, what most Senders do is mask their communication or wait until they see or hear some clue from the other person that makes them feel safe. Usually they are looking for the other person to say something simple like, "Hey, I like you a lot and I want to get to know you better." Now, this is something they can understand!

## Third-Party Verifiable: Another Super Important Concept

The ideal strategy for the Sender is to translate what s/he is thinking into Observable Behavior that is so clear and obvious that it becomes what we call in GHS, "Third-Party Verifiable." This means the Sender must place his/her personal thoughts and feelings, into words and/or actions so clearly, that their meaning is obvious. This step is also easier said than done. Let's look at some examples of "Third-Party Verifiable (TPV)."

**Example of Positive Third-Party Verifiable (TPV):**

Let us say you are hungry, and you recognize this inside your Inner Conversations. As a result, you say to your friend on the other side of the GAP, "I'm hungry. Let's find somewhere to eat."

This is clear communication by the Sender. You hear the Inner Conversation that your stomach tells your mind (Step One). You encode what your Inner Parent and Inner Child are saying into OB (Step Two), and then you make a Third-Party Verifiable communication to your friend (Step Three). Anyone listening to your communication would be able to recognize the following:

1) That you are hungry.
2) That you want to find somewhere to eat.

**Example of Negative Third-Party Verifiable (TPV):**

What if the Sender wasn't listening to his/her Inner Conversations? Inside their body is a cry of hunger from their stomach (Inner Child), but the Inner Parent isn't paying attention. All the Sender consciously feels is some vague discomfort. Skipping Step Two, the Sender says to the Receiver, "Hey, what do you want to do?"

In this case, neither the Receiver, nor an impartial jury of twelve witnesses, has any hope of understanding the true need of the Sender. We could guess or make up something, which is what we would have to do, as there is simply nothing solid to go on.

Is the Sender bored, or tired? Does s/he want to go somewhere? If so, where? He or she is not even putting the focus on his/her need when asking the other person, "What do you want to do?"

Let's say that the Receiver was your best friend and they knew you very well. S/he might ask, "Are you hungry?" You would then exclaim, "YES," since now the idea of hunger has been introduced into your conscious mind.

This is how many relationships work. A trial and error process occurs that, when it works, makes the relationship feel special. But let's say as a response your friend asked, "Do you want to see a movie?"

Now, the connection to your inner state would not be made. You then might start thinking about what movie you want to see, but your real goal might be to eat popcorn because you are so hungry.

What typically happens in most relationships is that the Sender, who is not really sure of what s/he is thinking and feeling, makes a vague stab at communicating his/her unmet need by saying something that really can't be defined or understood Third-Party Verifiably by the other person, the Receiver, or anyone else.

Before we go any further, let's take a closer look at this new term, Third-Party Verifiable. After this, we will discuss the role of the Receiver some more.

# {Ch 8} Third-Party Verifiability (TPV)

Let's devote this chapter to exploring the concept of Third-Party Verifiability. In many ways this is the ultimate concept in communication, since we can only evaluate or agree on what is being communicated by standards that are Third-Party Verifiable. Anything else is subjective or opinion.

The concept of Third-Party Verifiable is going to come up repeatedly once you've learned this topic. The more you try to figure out the source of communication problems, the more you are going to be asking yourself, "Is what this person trying to communicate Third-Party Verifiable?"

We need this concept of Third-Party Verifiability because there can easily be disagreement over the interpretation of what Observable Behavior means. It provides a standard by which successful communication can be assessed.

Let us say that the Observable Behavior (OB) might show one person punching another. At least two interpretations could come from this same OB. One is that the puncher is protecting or defending himself, the other is that the puncher is attacking the punched. Which one is correct? Since there can be varying interpretations of Observable Behavior, we will now introduce a test to determine when and if some OB is "Third-Party Verifiable."

## Third-Party Verifiable (TPV)

This term is destined to become a major part of your vocabulary when discussing the topic of communication. TPV describes a manner of interpreting what someone says or does, as objective observers would verify it.

In other words, if something is Third-Party Verifiable, this means that it could be clearly interpreted by either watching a video, listening to a recording, or getting the agreement of impartial witnesses. The video tape part is easy to understand. Take this sentence as an example:

"It was Third-Party Verifiable that Mary asked the store manager for her money back."

This sentence suggests if there was a video camera recording the conversation between Mary and the store manager, you could easily play back the part where Mary makes a statement asking for her money back.

### Another Example Might Be:

"It was not Third-Party Verifiable that Lisa apologized to John."

Even if a video camera were constantly filming a conversation between Lisa and John, during no part in the tape would there be a section that could be objectively interpreted as Lisa making an apology to John. Nothing was either said or seen that remotely suggested an apology.

Audio recordings work in the same manner. Let's say a person claims, "I never said that I would pay you the money back." If there was an audio recording of the phone conversation, and you can easily hear the distinctive voice of the person saying, "I will pay your money back." This means that the person's claim is NOT TPV.

What if there is no tape? We rarely have a camera recording all our words and actions during the day. This is why GHS has the test of Third-Party Verifiability, one that admittedly is subjective, but can be used to assess the situation. This is the aspect of "Third-Party Verifiable" that involves twelve impartial witnesses.

## Twelve Impartial Witnesses

This aspect of Third-Party Verifiable involves the mental concept of twelve impartial witnesses, much like jurors in a trial. Suppose that twelve people were watching the above video taped conversation between Mary and the store manager. If at least ten out of twelve of the witnesses agreed that Mary asked for her money back, then the decision is supported that it was Third-Party Verifiable that Mary asked for her money back.

If after watching the video tape less than ten out of twelve of the witnesses, perhaps even none of them, agree that Mary asked for her money back, this is definitely not Third-Party Verifiable.

This type of judgment becomes useful when there is no objective recording or written evidence to document a communication. In this case you must invoke the concept of impartial witnesses to imagine if the OB of the Sender "could" be determined objectively "if" there were external witnesses. This is less than impartial of course, but sometimes it is all you might have to make a determination.

This notion of Third-Party Verifiability is based on imagined neutral observers who must evaluate the same OB that you are seeing. This is particularly useful when you seek some distance from your personal opinion or strive to view a situation more objectively.

The idea is that impartial strangers would not have any personal knowledge of a specific person's thoughts and/or feelings. They can only interpret a communication based on what they are seeing or hearing for the first time when they don't know the person or situation at all.

If, based on what impartial observers could see and hear, they couldn't determine what a person was thinking or feeling, then the communication is not deemed TPV. If true, how can the intended Receiver be expected to interpret what the Sender is trying to say?

Practically speaking, this comes in handy in the following circumstances. We rarely have 6-12 impartial witnesses sitting around watching everything we say and do with another person. What the Third-Party Verifiable test does is help you to get outside your life-space to seek a detached assessment. Assuming no recordings are available, you just have to make your best deduction as to Third-Party Verifiability.

## How Does Third-Party Verifiability Protect the Sender as Well As The Receiver?

Suppose, a person in a private conversation states "how s/he feels" about something. Has s/he communicated her/his words in a way that is Third-Party Verifiable? Would a group of 6-12 strangers agree that the Sender's OB accurately reflects what s/he says that s/he thinks and feels? If so, then the Sender's communication is said to be Third-Party Verifiable. This is good!

If, on the other hand, 6-12 strangers could not agree to as to what the Sender says he thinks and feels, then his Observable Behavior is not Third-Party Verifiable. This is bad!

Third-Party Verifiability takes pressure off both the Sender and the Receiver, in that this test brings passable objectivity to interpreting the communication process.

If the Sender's communication is Third-Party Verifiable, then the communication problem is with the Receiver. If the Sender's communication is not Third-Party Verifiable, then the communication problem lies with the Sender.

Third-Party Verifiability represents an objective standard by which two (or more) people can assess communication across the GAP. Whoever is the most Third-Party Verifiable is given credit for communicating their true thoughts and feelings. It's quite possible that a Receiver doesn't truly want to hear the Sender's thoughts and feelings, but ultimately communication is based on giving and receiving honest messages.

Make no mistake, sooner or later some blame or judgment will need to be made. If there is a communication problem, getting to the win/win solution is going to take some investigation. If either Copartner is violating the GHS rules of communication (intended or not) then this is already a problem. These are the kinds of communication problems that ruin relationships.

## How Can TPV Help You Personally?

If you are experiencing conflict in an important relationship and things aren't going right, you may be blaming yourself when it might not be your fault. One thing you can always strive for in a relationship is to be as Third-Party Verifiable as possible with your communication. You would also strive for and seek the same with your relationship Copartners.

The marvelous thing about Third-Party Verifiability is that it can create objectivity. Whoever is Third-Party Verifiable can be understood by anyone who views that relationship interaction. Whoever is not Third-Party

Verifiable, will confuse anyone viewing the relationship, including the participants.

## Is Third-Party Verifiability A Perfect System?

Third-Party Verifiability is not a perfect system, but it is the best we have. The essence of communication is sharing truthfully and with integrity what you think and feel. Having your communication interpreted accurately on the other side of the GAP is equally a part of this equation.

As a student of Generic Human Studies, you will strive to communicate your unmet needs, based on your genuine thoughts and feelings from your side of the GAP. You will be watchful that the Observable Behavior you send from your side of the GAP to your various Receivers will be as 3PV as possible. You will also be assessing the 3PV of your Copartner's responses by paying attention to what s/he says/does, so you correctly interpret the thoughts and feelings behind their OB.

Third-Party verifiability presents an impartial test to seek objectivity when evaluating a communication problem. TPV is the ideal way to evaluate communication so the Two-Copartners can stop arguing endlessly between themselves about what "he said/she said."

Third-Party verifiability determines if what a person says s/he "thinks and feels" is supported by actual behavior (words and deeds) that accurately communicates their thoughts and feelings.

By adhering to standards that can be objectively verified, the cause of a communication problem between Two-Copartners can be quickly discovered and easily resolved.

Very often a Copartner will have strong thoughts and feelings inside his/her mind, but these are not enough to be Third-Party Verifiable. If a person does not properly translate his/her deeply held thoughts and feelings into suitable words or actions, this person's communication is non-Third-Party Verifiable.

If a person says s/he has thoughts and feelings of a certain nature, but words or actions (OB) do not back her/him up, how is the Receiver (or any other third-party observers) going to know for certain if those feelings and thoughts are sincere?

Occasionally, you will have the opportunity to ask a more objective person or group of people their opinion of what certain words and actions mean based on hearing them. This can be a very instructive experience. It is amazing how TPV Third-Party Verifiability can be when it's put to the test.

## TPV: A Practical Example

Let's use an example from a Husband/Wife relationship. Suppose a husband has loving thoughts and feelings for his wife. He is experiencing these thoughts and feelings of love inside his mind and he wants to communicate them to his wife. He decides to translate these thoughts and feelings into Observable Behavior so he can share them with his spouse. While saying "I love you" the husband concurrently caresses the hand of his wife in a soft, gentle manner while looking directly into her eyes.

In this situation, an impartial panel of judges watching a video tape of the OB would agree that the husband spoke the words "I love you" and that he performed the actions of caressing his wife's hand in a soft, gentle manner. Since most people would agree that these words and deeds genuinely represent the internal thoughts and feelings of "I love you," an impartial panel of judges would say the same thing.

Therefore, the husband's claim, that he had thoughts and feelings of love for his wife, would be considered TPV. He did indeed accurately translate his thoughts and feelings of love for his wife into OB that was TPV.

### Thoughts and Feelings That Are Not Third-Party Verifiable

Imagine a different husband who says that he has loving thoughts and feelings for his wife who also makes the claim that he communicates this regularly to his wife. But if a video camera were watching him all day, it would record the OB of the husband watching television all day without saying or doing anything with or to his wife at all.

In this instance, the husband's alleged thoughts and feelings are not Third Party verifiable. A video camera would not pick up any words or actions that could be interpreted by others as being thoughts or feelings of love for his wife.

An impartial panel of witnesses would have no basis for interpreting the husband's behavior as being loving towards his wife. No matter how strong the husband's internal beliefs and feelings of love, there is no third-party verifiability for his statement, "I love my wife."

The impartial panel of judges might decide, or the video camera might show, some physical signs that suggest the husband is having intense thoughts or feelings, but about what? The game on television...? Life in general...? Who knows...? Any interpretation would only be a wild guess. The first example meets the criterion of being TPV, the second example does not.

## Applying the Test of Third-Party Verifiability

Suppose, using the first example, the wife is accusing her husband of not loving her. She insists that her husband doesn't love her at all. The husband could remind his wife about his Third-Party Verifiable behaviors in his defense.

But since she already doesn't believe him after having experienced the TPV behavior for herself, this is unlikely to be successful. Even though the husband may not be able to convince his wife, he would have impartial strangers believe him because his actions were and are TPV.

Here is the important part! Even if his wife remains unconvinced, the husband can be sure of one fact. His inability to communicate his thoughts and feelings to his wife across the GAP is not his fault. She is the one with a problem of interpretation on her side of the GAP! Despite the fact that his actions are "TPV", his wife cannot accept this communication because of a problem she has on her side of the GAP.

## How Is the Protection of Third-Party Verifiability Crucial to The Husband in This Example?

In this situation, the test of Third-Party verifiability is crucial to the mind-set of the husband because he may start to feel upset or find fault with his own self-esteem or actions. Even though he knows he has accurately communicated his thoughts and feelings, he may begin to feel upset or experience self-doubt because his wife has not received or validated his feelings. Not knowing about third-party verifiability, he might even blame himself or feel inadequate in some way. He could start disbelieving himself or even his feelings for his wife.

With third-party verifiability on his side, he can at least take comfort that he has objective verification that he does indeed feel the way he says he does about his wife. This takes the pressure off the husband and puts the responsibility on his wife for not being able to accurately interpret or accept his TPV communications. Naturally this example could just as easily be reversed between the husband and wife or extrapolated to any role in any of the 12-Human Relationships.

## What Will Third-Party Verifiability Show?

Third-Party Verifiability will show which side of the communication is causing the clash. Is it the Sender who is not translating his/her thoughts and feelings into accurate and identifiable OB, or is it the Receiver who is not interpreting the OB in a way accepted by most people?

Third-Party Verifiability is a neutral concept; it supports whoever is creating clear and understandable communication and exposes those who do not. When both Copartners are communicating in an equally TPV manner, the relationship has a much stronger chance to achieve win/win outcomes.

The concept of Third-Party Verifiability helps any Copartner who cares about the quality of his/her relationships to study and improve their communication methods. It helps him/her to understand more of what is happening with a communication problem. This is incredibly valuable and may be the only solace that a Copartner has in his/her defense.

Third-Party Verifiability is particularly effective, when both Copartners in a relationship work together to make all their communications as TPV as possible. When this happens, any problem relationship will quickly improve. Win/Win relationships are the natural and realistic result of such a cooperative union.

You will now start to see many examples of Third-Party Verifiability being, or not being present. Now that you know the concept of TPV, you will discover examples and applications everywhere; in books, movies, television, plays, and even in your own relationships.

Although it's incredibly important, TPV is not the sole criterion that creates relationship problems. There can be problems involving any aspect of the Environment, Structure, or Two-Copartners in a relationship. However, Third-Party Verifiable is at the core of many relationship difficulties and can be corrected once studied and applied by willing Copartners.

So far, we've been describing the role of the Sender when communicating. However, this reflects only one half of the seesaw dynamics. It turns out the Receiver side has just as much importance when it comes to a quality exchange between Two-Copartners.

Even if the Sender is "perfectly TPV" with his/her communication and OB, the Receiver still has a role to play in receiving and interpreting the communication as it was sent. Next, we will explore the Receiver's side of communication.

# {Ch 9} The Receiver Side of Communication

What's next? We have discussed the Sender. Is this all we need for communication to occur? If we perfectly send a message as the Sender don't you think that should be enough? Not yet! Even so, in many communication books and studies it often appears that only the Sender's role is deemed important. It's as if the Receiver's role is supposed to happen automagically. Not so.

Now we are going to learn how the Receiver's role is every bit as crucial as the Sender's to achieve positive communication. Assume for the moment, that:

- The Sender is aware of his/her true thoughts and feelings.
- The Sender encodes them in a perfect, Third-Party Verifiable manner.
- The Sender sends his/her OB easily and smoothly across the GAP.

Now let's observe from the other side of the seesaw. Even if the relationship Sender does an excellent job of translating his/her thoughts and feelings into OB (so perfect that it's even TPV), there is still more to the communication equation. The Receiver has an equally important part to play on his/her side of the GAP.

## Who Is the Receiver?

First let's define, who is the Receiver? The Receiver is the person to whom the Sender is wanting to communicate his/her need. For this explanation, let's assume that you are now on the Receiver side of the relationship. We continue the numbering started in the Sender section because this really is Step 4 of the 6-part communication sequence.

### Role of The Receiver

The role of the Receiver in communication is to:

Step 4. Be paying attention to the Sender so that she/he can see and/or hear what the Sender says and does.

Step 5. Be able to correctly interpret the Observable Behavior of the Sender with a accurate assessment of his/her thoughts and feelings

Step 6. Respond appropriately to the Sender's communication.

Let's look at each of these three aspects of the Receiver role.

## Step 4: Paying Attention

For a communication to be received, there must be a person who is paying attention to or in a position to receive any message that is being sent. This means that the Receiver is aware enough of the Sender to catch what he/she might say or do relative to your relationship.

The first major communication problem on the receiving side occurs if the Receiver is simply not paying attention to the Sender. This may be unintentional on the part of the Receiver. Perhaps, his/her attention is elsewhere, focused on the Internet or television. Perhaps the Receiver is having a crisis on his/her own side of the GAP that the Sender does not know about. If the Receiver is not able, or simply not paying attention, communication is blocked right there. The message being sent has no possibility of being received.

Another factor on the Receiver side is that the Sender may not be speaking loudly enough or be facing in a direction that makes the words difficult to hear. However, let's assume the Receiver is paying attention and is in a position to receive the Sender's message.

The next step is to make an accurate interpretation of the Sender's OB. In the same way that the Sender must "encode" her/his thoughts and feelings into Observable Behavior, the Receiver must now "decode" the OB to decide what the Sender's thoughts and feelings might be.

## Step 5: The Receiver Must Make an Accurate Interpretation of the Sender's Observable Behavior

Once the Sender's words and actions are seen and/or heard, the Receiver's role is to correctly interpret the meaning of the Sender's Observable Behavior.

As mentioned above, the technical term for this step on the Receiver side is called "decoding." Once the Sender's thoughts and feelings are received across the GAP, the Receiver must now interpret based on the OB, what makes the most sense to explain the Sender's unmet need.

This involves at least four potential scenarios.

### The Sender's OB is not 3PV and Can't Be Understood

In this case there is just no way of knowing what need the Sender is asking to be met. This is the Sender's fault. What the Sender is encoding, is impossible to interpret by any Third-Party Verifiable standard. If this is true, the Receiver is off the hook for not understanding the unmet need being communicated.

### The Sender's OB is 3PV but Misinterpreted

It is certainly possible that the Receiver could make a wrong interpretation of the Sender's Observable Behavior on his/her side of the GAP, even if it's fully TPV. Here the Sender's attempt at communication is still never realized but this is the Receiver's fault. Ideally this doesn't happen too often and is quickly corrected.

This step can be frustrating for the Sender, since the interpretation of her/his Observable Behavior is completely out of the Sender's hands as it is taking place on the other side of the seesaw.

**The Sender's OB is 3PV AND Interpreted Correctly**

In this case the Receiver is easily able to decode and understand the OB along with the intent of the Sender. The Sender has encoded her/his internal thoughts and feelings into words or actions that were easy to see or hear. Inside the Receiver's mind, s/he is able to interpret the OB into thoughts and feelings that communicate the most logical meaning based on the situation.

**The Sender's OB is not 3PV and yet is Interpreted Correctly**

Even if the Senders OB is not 3PV, the Receiver may still successfully interpret the unmet need for which the Sender is communicating. Mothers do this all the time with their children. A person who is naturally empathic can often interpret vague OB and be 100% correct in assessing the need of the Sender. This is great when it happens, but it's not good to rely on this as a long-term strategy.

**Figuring out the need of a Sender has many different levels.**

Sometimes it is easy to know what a Sender is saying. S/he is clear, to the point, and the message is Third-Party verifiable. Other times, you may have no idea what the person is saying because neither does the Sender. The job of the Receiver is to decipher what the unmet need might be and then if possible, respond appropriately. To do this effectively it's always helpful to keep in mind that your Sender has an unmet need.

Problems that occur on the receiving side of the seesaw are entirely different from the problems of the Sender. They involve the Receiver's skill to accurately interpreting the Sender's Observable Behavior.

A classic example is the guy acting as the Sender, who tells the girl he has just started dating that he doesn't want to settle down in any one relationship. What the girl hears as the Receiver inside her own mind, is that she can change what he is saying into what she wants, which is for him to marry her. What objective observers hear is this guy is not even looking for a permanent girlfriend.

In this case, the Sender's communication does not cross the GAP because the Receiver is misinterpreting it.

## Step 6: The Receiver Responds Appropriately

Assuming the Receiver is paying attention and correctly interprets the well-formed OB of the Sender, the sixth (and final) function to complete the communication is for the Receiver to respond appropriately.

This could take place in a variety of ways. If the Sender said s/he was thirsty, the Receiver could offer them a drink. If the Sender was asking for directions, the Receiver could give the person a map or offer to write down directions or look them up on a computer. If the person was sobbing over the loss of a loved one, s/he could just be there silently for the person in an empathic manner.

Responding appropriately represents the art of communication. Sometimes just listening, accepting, and responding with a nod or a look is the most appropriate response. It could also simply be the touch of a hand.

Being able to listen to something difficult the Sender is expressing without automatically starting to pontificate an inappropriate response can be quite a wonder for the Sender. The better a Receiver is at responding appropriately, the better the whole communication exchange is going to be.

During the average day to day, back and forth of "normal" communication, the most appropriate response is often simply making the switch of converting to the Sender role. This occurs when offering an additional comment or observation that furthers the ongoing conversation.

## Summarizing the Steps of Communication

Let's review the paired roles of the Sender and Receiver. The major challenge of communicating as a Sender (a three-step process) is to:

1. Be in touch with a Personal (PEM), and/or Relational (FSW) need.
2. Encode his/her personal thoughts and feelings into Observable Behavior that reflects the unmet need in Third-Party Verifiable way.
3. Send this unmet need as OB effectively across the GAP.

The biggest challenge of communicating as a Receiver (also a three-step process) is to

4. Be paying attention to the Sender.
5. Accurately interpret the Sender's Observable Behavior as expressing her/his personal thoughts and feelings (an unmet need), and
6. Responding appropriately to the Sender's communication.

# {Ch 10} Communication: Possible Problems w/ the 6-Steps

We are now going to combine the 6 steps as outlined previously into one unit and call it "a message." This is an obvious word, but it hasn't been mentioned until now for a reason. When communication is flowing freely and working well, then it's simply a series of well-constructed messages that are sent and received back and forth between the Two-Copartners on their appropriate relationship seesaw.

When best friends are conversing, there's simply an easy flow of messages that alternate quite naturally between Sender and Receiver with rarely a missed communication or problem. Here we simply refer to the 6-Steps as a message, so we don't have to keep referring to 6-Steps all the time.

However, if dealing with a sticky communication problem at its very core, you may find it necessary to parse each step of the message to determine which step is not flowing correctly. You are now familiar with these steps, but let's take a moment to review them one more time.

Here is a review of each steps that completes a one-way message from Sender to Receiver.

## The 6-Steps Communication Process (One-Way)

Step 1. The Sender becomes aware of thoughts and feelings (reflecting an unmet need) that s/he wants to communicate to the Receiver.

Step 2. The Sender accurately encodes his/her internal thoughts and feelings into external words or actions (Observable Behavior)

Step 3. The Sender sends OB that travels across the GAP in a Third-Party Verifiable manner.

Step 4. The Receiver is paying attention to the Sender's Observable Behavior (words or actions) and thus sees and hears the Sender's OB.

Step 5. The Receiver decodes the Sender's OB accurately as thoughts and/or feelings s/he understands in his/her mind.

Step 6. The Sender responds appropriately as s/he feels fits the situation.

These steps reflect a one-way message. Think of it like a game of catch. The Sender throws the ball and the Receiver catches it. When the ball is caught Steps 4 and 5 are completed. In step 6 the Receiver may "throw the ball back" by choosing to respond with a new communication and thus become the Sender who starts a new message having 6-steps.

In "normal" conversations lots of messages are exchanged back and forth. Both Sender and Receiver switch roles, so two-way communication can occur. This happens quite easily and naturally in the "real world," especially in relationships with people we like and are close to.

We never worry or even think about these 6-steps. This is what communication professors mean when they say that just like a fish is surrounded by water, we are surrounded by communication. During arguments and heated discussions however, these 6-Steps can get submerged when the emotions take over.

Even without emotions or conflict, problems can easily occur at any of the steps. What goes wrong in tense situations is that these steps get missed or don't happen. If you are paying attention, it's relatively easy to determine which step did not complete properly.

The purpose of this chapter is to show some potential ways that these 6-Steps can be disrupted. It certainly won't have ALL the ways this can happen, but you'll see there is a nice collection of the types of problems to watch for. If they happen to you in your relationships you won't be happy about it, unless and until the situation is resolved.

## Problems That Occur in Relationships with the Communication Process

Communication in your various relationships typically revolves around the relationship structure you are on with the person. Once you know this, you will have a clearer idea of the standard topics for discussion. At work you talk mostly about work topics, with social relationships you discuss your social interactions, etc. Family relationships can pretty much revolve around any topic important to the family members.

Even when you completely understand your relationship anatomy, problems can still occur at each of the 6-Steps. You can evaluate any message by focusing on how it fulfils each step. The trouble being that "normal" communication typically takes place with a brisk back and forth action.

This makes it challenging to track each of the six steps in a routine conversation, not to mention during something more intense like an argument. And if it's a Work or Professional relationship, there can be additional emotional weight or responsibility to the messages being sent and received.

You don't even need to be in a tense situation or an argument for pitfalls to occur. Given that most of us are not trained in these 6-Steps, you may recognize some of the following classic problems that might crop up at each of these six steps. The following is a list of each step along with some potential problems that might occur.

### Step 1: The Sender Becomes Aware of Thoughts or Feelings

Often the person who desires to communicate is unaware of what s/he is truly thinking and feeling. They may have a general idea, but not a specific awareness. If one is unclear about what s/he is thinking and feeling, it is very difficult to translate this into accurate Observable Behavior. Often Senders move directly into words and actions before they even have internally defined the purpose or goal of their communication.

They may experience some vague discomfort and immediately start talking just to make the feeling go away. They may have no clue as to what they are experiencing on the inside that motivates these feelings. Even if they do, they may disguise what they want, experience, or feel for reasons such as embarrassment, not wanting to intrude, or to conceal their motivation. They could experience a variety of reasons causing them to disguise their true thoughts or concerns.

Every person has a distinctive style by which they approach and understand their personal needs. This would have been established growing up during their early family years and be heavily influenced by external forces. Most people would have a passable grasp on their main personal, emotional, or mental needs. However, these patterns can become distorted if stress takes over, such as meeting someone you suddenly care about or starting a new school or job.

When getting to know new people, they tend to hide or disguise their true motivations and communication style. Getting to know a person over time is the only way for you to accurately learn how good your Copartner will be at self-identifying their various needs and concerns. The applies most specifically to new Social and Work relationships as you have certainly gotten to know your close Family members.

**Step 2: The Sender Translates His/Her Thoughts and Feelings into Words or Actions (Observable Behavior).**

When the words and actions begin with any person is when the communication begins. Since words and actions are the only thing a Receiver can see and hear, they should be chosen with care so that they accurately reflect what you are thinking and feeling.

Many people use words and actions that are extremely poor indicators of what they are actually thinking and feeling. Or, what they are thinking and feeling is so negative they simply don't want to say. Or, they think that the Receiver is not supposed to know what they are truly thinking/feeling. This hides or distorts the true message before the Receiver even has a chance to make a decoding mistake.

Another possibility that prevents the Sender's OB from being TPV could be complex actions. For example, someone you know is crying. You recognize something could be wrong, but you don't know what. S/he may even be crying for joy. The crying is OB, but it may not clearly establish the cause for the underlying emotion.

Another possible flaw is that the Sender provides clear OB, but for a false reason. For example, the Sender might give a direction in clear terms as to why they want to go somewhere. But they don't tell the Receiver the genuine reason. They might not even know the true reason, but they resort to a default behavior or excuse they know will work to get out of a situation.

**Step 3: The Observable Behavior Is Sent Across the Gap.**

This step can become a transmission problem such as when talking on the telephone and the line goes dead or sending a letter or package that is never received, or an email that goes into spam and is deleted. Accurate OB that perfectly reflects your thoughts and feelings can be drowned out by airplane noise or a train going by.

There could be many possibilities that make the transfer of OB across the GAP problematic. And when the Sender has accurately sent what s/he was thinking and feeling across the GAP, s/he may believe that communication has occurred even though it was never accurately received.

What happens when Copartner A writes and mails a letter that Copartner B never receives? Yes, Copartner A has expressed their need to communicate; s/he has sent clear thoughts and feelings across the GAP. But not until Copartner B opens, reads and understands the letter, has the message truly been received.

How many movies have you seen where the written message falls behind the desk, or comes off the door where it was pinned, and the plot twists as a result of the missed communication? Maybe you even have a story of a missed communication from your own life.

### Step 4: The Receiver Pays Attention

This step should be pretty straightforward. What a person says or does is so obvious that it could easily be documented by a camcorder. But suppose the Receiver is not paying attention for some reason, or can't hear the Sender, or is preoccupied ordering a hamburger. This means, even with excellent Sender dynamics, the Receiver is not in position to receive the communication as it crosses the GAP.

If something goes wrong at this step, it is due to the faulty reception (of the Sender's words or deeds) by the Receiver. Technically the communication traveled across the GAP but was missed by the Receiver during Step 4. Copartner A's message must be accurately received by Copartner B before communication takes place.

### Step 5: The Receiver Interprets the Sender's Observable Behavior

A problem with this step might be the Receiver clearly receives the Sender's words and actions, but his/her interpretation is wrong. Perhaps the two speakers are from different cultures, and the same hand gestures have different meanings to each.

What if a Sender makes a very clear statement that the Receiver simply doesn't want to hear? The Receiver could block it out mentally or reinterpret the meaning completely. What if the Receiver doesn't have the experience to correctly interpret the Sender's words? Perhaps the Sender is using slang or professional terms, such as between a doctor and patient.

This step implies that the Receiver has an obligation to try to correctly interpret the Sender's intention. If the Receiver is not reasonably clear, it's their duty to ask for clarification. Sometimes this is not possible or is made difficult by the Sender's attitude. Whatever the cause might be, if the Receiver's interpretation is incorrect as per the intention of the Sender, then the message does not get through.

### Step 6: The Receiver Responds Appropriately

Have you ever expressed a genuine need to someone from your side of the GAP and had him/her respond as if living in an alternate universe? Welcome to the world of miscommunication. This happens sometimes.

The Receiver is on the other side of the seesaw. S/he is living in his/her domain and can act however they want. If a Receiver doesn't respond the way you would like, this is unfortunate. You have no control over that side of the seesaw, nor would you want it.

The skill of the Receiver to respond appropriately represents the true art of communication. The end goal of Step 6 has various options:

- Not responding at all, with OB or otherwise.
- Responding with OB that says the message was received but with no additional response.
- Responding with a new message related to the Sender's original message.

- Responding with a new message totally unrelated to the prior message, also known as "changing the subject."

How a Receiver responds can stop the communication dead in its tracks or invite the next round of messages. Depending on how s/he handles the original message could determine various outcomes of which there are too many to mention.

## GAP Issues

Problems can also occur because there is more than one kind of GAP. In most cases, the GAP is simply the physical space between the Two-Copartners who want to communicate. However, there may also be a psychological gap of understanding between two people, called the "Awareness GAP."

Using a prior example, suppose one Copartner is a doctor and the other is the patient. The doctor may be explaining a medical procedure using terminology the patient simply can't understand because the patient doesn't have a background in medicine. (It may be excellent communication if the Receiver was also a doctor.) In this situation clear communication does not occur because of an "Awareness GAP." Another might be asking a tech support question and getting back a technical answer that has little relevance to the actual problem.

The Awareness GAP can occur in any situation where one person has more knowledge about a topic than another. A runner is trying to explain "carbohydrate loading" to his mother. An office worker is attempting to explaining the new communication network to her hairdresser.

Maharishi Mahesh Yogi, the famous guru of the Beatles, spoke to this Awareness GAP from another perspective. His quote was, "The words of the teacher are heard on the level of the student." This illustrates that a teacher's level of understanding (awareness GAP) on a topic differs immensely from the student's ability to comprehend the same topic. This is simply because the student doesn't have the same depth of subjective experience.

Another quote, this time from Einstein, is also an example of the potential of an "Awareness Gap." Einstein once said to his students after a lecture, "If you understood me, then I haven't been clear."

A final example of this phenomena is that I guarantee that your Awareness GAP of the material in this book will be vastly less after reading it for a second time after experimenting with and applying its principles to your relationships in the "real world."

**What Is "Crossing the Gap?"**

Another common and potent killer of communication is especially important to avoid. You do not want to be on the Sending or Receiving side when someone "crosses the Gap." Let me explain.

What would happen if you were sitting comfortably on a seesaw with someone and you crawled over to their side? The seesaw stops working doesn't it; typically, by crashing hard to the ground! It also works the same way if that person crosses over to your side as well.

In communication "Crossing the GAP" takes the form of telling the person on their side of the seesaw, "This is what and how you are supposed to think and feel." Doing this while conversing means you have no concern or value for the other person's side of the seesaw. This is not a good way to foster communication.

What you are actually doing when you "cross the GAP" is depriving them of their autonomy to run and operate their side of the seesaw as they see fit. They "own" their side of the seesaw, so to speak. They have the right and responsibility to operate their side. If you attempt to start doing or making decisions for him/her, then you are "crossing the GAP." You always want to do your best to refrain from "crossing the GAP" as well as be on the lookout that it doesn't happen to you.

Crossing the GAP can take many forms and is always a deterrent to the communication process. You may think you know what a person's need is, you may feel you know exactly what a person is feeling, and you may be right. Nevertheless, the other side of the GAP is the other person's domain, responsibility, and obligation.

Your role, as the Sender is to place your communication into OB that is easy to interpret. Your role as the Receiver, when you are not sure of a communication, is to ask for clarification. Whichever side of the seesaw you are on, you are not inside that person's heart and mind. If you start "acting for the other person" on their side, communication has ended right there.

A common Receiver problem is to think that s/he already knows what the Sender is trying to communicate. This alone causes major problems. Even if you are certain for a fact you know what a person is thinking or feeling, you are much better off to ask, "ARE you thinking and feeling such and such?" rather than assuming you absolutely know what they are experiencing. You might be surprised what you find out.

From the Sender's side "crossing the Gap' occurs when s/he explains to the Receiver how s/he is to act or feel. Doing this, they disregard whatever the Receiver is actually experiencing and simply give instructions s/he is supposed to follow. This is typically not behavior the Receiver appreciates.

**What Is "Ascribing?"**

Another form of "crossing the GAP" occurs via a process GHS calls "ascribing." As you learn increasingly more about GHS communication, you'll find you'll need to constantly be on guard for people who are crossing the GAP with you by ascribing thoughts and feelings to your OB which you may not find exactly accurate.

They are not telling you *what* to think and feel. They are incorrectly deciding what they *think* you are thinking and feeling. Then they respond to their incorrect assumption, as if it was something you actually did say or intend.

This derails your interaction entirely. When you become excellent at communication you will spot this instantly.

Another version is that from their receiving side of the seesaw they think they already know what you are feeling or wanting to say. So, they begin acting as if this information is true, even though they haven't even bothered to check this with you. "You must be angry, you must be happy, of course you are disappointed, etc."

Once you learn and practice how "not to cross the GAP" from your side of the seesaw, you will find that others do this much more frequently than you ever imagined. You won't like it when it happens to you, so avoid doing it to others. You'll learn to recognize and protect yourself from ascribing as much as possible.

**What Is the Best Way Not To "Cross The GAP"?**

Let's suppose that you know and believe 100% that you know what your friend is thinking or feeling. Before acting on this, do the following. Check your assumption out by asking him or her, "Are you thinking and feeling __________?

Don't be surprised if their response is to say, "No" or they want to clarify what you just said. If they agree 100%, then that is okay as well. No harm done. But if you were wrong, you'll be happy you asked.

You may think you know what a person's need is, you may feel certain that you know what a person is feeling, and you may even be right. Nevertheless, the other side of the GAP is the other person's responsibility. You are not inside that person's heart and mind. Your role, as the Receiver is to ask if you are correct. Asking for confirmation from your relationship Copartner is the best and easiest way to never cross the GAP.

As you learn more about GHS communication, you will also find yourself needing to be constantly on guard for people who are crossing the GAP with you. You may find them making a misguided point to you when you are attempting to share with them. You'll catch the situation because it changes the tone of the conversation. It will be easy to spot once you've experienced this a few times.

Ideally, you never want to cross the GAP, nor do you want someone with whom you are in a relationship to cross the GAP. Some people operate most of their relationships by crossing the GAP on a regular basis. This is their total strategy.

## How Does "Crossing the GAP," Relate to the "Mid-Gap Line"?

The Mid-Gap Line is the balance point or fulcrum of a seesaw. If one person on the seesaw goes past the midpoint, the seesaw will crash on that side.

When involved in a relationship each Copartner must strive never to extend their energy past the Mid-Gap Line. Once a person goes past the Mid-Gap point, s/he, by definition, is using their own personal energy to supplant the energy of the person on the other side.

Going past the Mid-Gap Line in the Seesaw Analogy puts the Copartner on the other side of the seesaw 's fulcrum (mid-gap point) trying with great difficulty to work both sides of the seesaw (relationship) at the same time.

Two-Copartners on one side of a seesaw, a relationship does not make. - Yoda.

The key to successful relationships is to take responsibility for your personal half of the relationship seesaw up to the Mid-Gap Line. When your Copartner does the same, your relationship has a much better chance to balance and perform correctly.

One interesting way to make this point is to state that as an individual, you have 100% responsibility for your 50% side of a relationship seesaw. In terms of SELF-Parenting, your Inner Parent and Inner Child share 50% responsibility each for their 100% share of their 50% share of an outer relationship seesaw. You're welcome!

# {Ch 11} What Is A Person's Life-Space?

Another term used in GHS is Life-Space. A person's Life-Space is what s/he is thinking and feeling. The key thing about a person's Life-Space is that it exists wholly within his/her body, heart, and mind; therefore, it is not truly knowable (nor can it be directly experienced) by another. Thus, it exists solely within the private domain of each person.

Everything we might surmise about a person's Life-Space is based on interpretation. It is impossible to prove what is in a person's Life-space because there is no externally objective way to look inside a person's Life-space.

Being on the outside we are essentially guessing what a person truly thinks and feels. If a person is highly aware of his/her personal thoughts and feelings and is honest and trustworthy, then you can confirm over time if what they tell you accurately reflects his/her Life-Space.

Just because a person tells you s/he is thinking and feeling a certain way, doesn't make it so. If the person is unaware of his/her own thoughts and feelings and/or is dishonest, then you can never be sure that what they tell you is an honest reflection of his/her Life-Space.

## Why Is the Term Life-Space Used in Generic Human Studies?

The term, Life-Space, clarifies a point when discussing relationship communication. A person's Life-space holds his/her thoughts and feelings. There is no direct way of looking inside a person's mind to truly know what s/he is thinking or feeling. This is processing that takes place inside his/her own heart and mind. Even if someone tells us how or what s/he is feeling or thinking, they could be lying. And it truly is amazing how good some people are at lying.

Each person is the owner of their own personal Life-space which includes thoughts and feelings that are distinct from what we can see and hear as Observable Behavior. Our only way of interpreting the thoughts and feelings in someone's Life-Space is by their OB. And this is still an interpretation.

## What Does A Person's Life-Space Create in The Communication Process?

Each person's life-space creates a point of view on his or her side of the GAP. This point of view is what separates the Two-Copartners sitting across from each other on the seesaw. The Copartner roles in a relationship represent the energy source by which each Copartner can meet his/her needs in a relationship. Here are two examples.

### Boss and Employee Points of View

A Boss and Employee will always have an opposing perspective in their relationship even though they may be able to see each other's point of view and agree on certain circumstances. It is an inherent function of their Life-Space. If the same two people switch roles on the B/E seesaw, they will then adopt the point of view of their new role.

The Boss is going to be concerned with the function of the job. They will want to know whether the Employee is up to the task, will arrive on time, will give their best effort, etc. The Employee will be leery of being overworked by the Boss, underpaid, working under harsh conditions, etc.

### Boyfriend/Girlfriend Points of View

Let's assume a new Boyfriend/Girlfriend Relationship where the girlfriend has an old boyfriend who she has broken up with, but still wants to see socially, "as a friend." Her viewpoint as the new girlfriend is going to be different from her new boyfriend's. She's going to say that seeing her old boyfriend "socially" is totally fine.

Friends of this girl who are not in this situation can often be objective and sympathetic to their girlfriend when asked their opinion about such a situation. However, if one of those girlfriends finds herself in the reverse position in which her new boyfriend has an old girlfriend he wants to keep seeing "as a friend," she won't like it at all.

It's amazing how playing the opposite role on a relationship seesaw can change a person's life-space to take on another perspective. There are 12 generic human relationships for a total of 24 potential roles. Each Role on the relationship seesaw provides the rules and customs that govern and shape the performance of the person playing that role. This is why it's important to understand each role in a relationship.

The Role is a model of behavior. The person playing the Role is the actor assigned to that role. If they don't perform the role properly or try to act based on rules associated with another role, then problems develop. When communication problems are extensive, then it typically points to a greater problem with the role, or the person playing the role.

## What Social Factors Contribute to A Person's Life-Space?

Many social factors contribute to the perspective of a person's Life-Space (thoughts and feelings). Some examples are: family background, birth order, gender, age, ethnic origin, neighborhood, religion, occupation of parents, financial resources or lack thereof, physical health, social status, education, political opinions, interests such as hobbies and sports, marital status, physical characteristics, personality, temperament, maturity, sexual preference, intelligence, attitudes towards sex, gender, race, religion, and politics, and the list goes on.

Any one of the above factors can trigger a completely different Life/Space perspective, even if two people are similar in most other ways. Everyone is an individual within his/her own Life-Space. This is the foundation for why such a variety of interactions can occur, even if most of the external circumstances of a relationship are absolutely similar.

### When Does Generic Human Studies Consider A Person Responsible for His/Her Personal Life-Space?

From the GHS perspective, when a person reaches the age of 18, s/he is given the mantle of responsibility for his/her own Life-Space circumstances. This includes the meeting or non-meeting of his/her personal:

- Physical needs
- Emotional needs
- Mental needs

This also includes the Relational worlds in which they find themselves as regards their:

- Family Relationships
- Social Relationships
- Work Relationships
- Professional Relationships

Once the person is 18, it's just an arbitrary point in time where they are deemed responsible or "in charge of" their own Life-Space. Of course, there may be extenuating circumstances. This is simply a marker for reference.

# {Ch 12} Problem-Solving Difficult Relationships

## One Key Factor for Resolving Difficult Relationships (Plus Another)

Unfortunately, there is One Key Factor you must understand before seeking to solve any relationship problem. It pains me to have to reveal this to you at this stage because ideally, excellent communication would be able to save or solve any relationship problem. Yet, such is not the case.

This next truth makes the idea of your having any "control" over a relationship a virtual impossibility. The reality of this truth has always been implicit in the system, but to see it expressed with these next simple words is strong medicine for what is regrettably a condition that cannot be cured. Here it is.

*You can be 100% perfect from your side of any relationship seesaw, yet your relationship can still fail miserably.* The reason is as follows. *For any Outer Relationship you only control one-half of the seesaw structure.*

As mentioned earlier, each Copartner enjoys 100% responsibility for his/her half (50%) side of the seesaw. However, if for ANY reason, the other person no longer wants to participate, s/he can jump off the seesaw and there is nothing you can do about it. Also, if a person refuses to "act right" on his/her side of the seesaw, there is nothing you can legitimacy do about this either.

This assumes that you are unwilling to do anything that would force the person to comply or go against their will. Karmically speaking, this is the right decision, as painful as it may feel to not control both sides of a seesaw to your liking.

If you can establish a relationship where your Copartner is 100% willing to be responsible for his/her own lifespace and let you do the same, you have an excellent chance for a successful win/win relationship. This is based on being able to work out any communication issues such as outlined in this book.

However, there is another factor which is no less important, that can doom a relationship to failure even if both Copartners are totally giving 100% from their 50% side of the seesaw and communicating perfectly. It's a bit hidden in the system, so it's also worth a warning in case it happens to you, which it probably will at some point in your life.

## Problems Caused by The Environment

The Environment also plays a crucial and pivotal role in regulating various relationship interactions. If the Environment somehow changes, it can cause the relationship to end even if both people otherwise would have wanted to keep it going with 100% commitment.

One example might be when two people in a relationship live in the same city, perhaps as friends, neighbors, or a romantic couple. Their relationship is really positive. Then, for some reason, some aspect of their external environment changes, for example one of them loses their job, or graduates from college, or some other external factor such as a family death or natural disaster occurs. Now one or both Copartners have to move, and this causes the relationship to be shattered despite the best intentions of both.

These are extreme examples, but you do need to understand this potential reality. You may perform your side of a relationship seesaw with the purest intentions possible. Yet this relationship can still fail or be irretrievably altered due to something out of your control.

For the next set of "relationship problems" let' assume both Copartners want a relationship to continue and the Environment is supportive of their interaction. Even given these ideal circumstances, you could have "real world" problems. This takes the theory of how communication works and moves it up a notch much like climbing a real mountain after taking a basic bouldering course in the foothills.

Only personal "real world" experience will teach you how communication works in "real world" situations. Here is where you begin to apply these principles in action. Let's visit an earlier analogy.

If you want to be able to "heal the body," first you need to learn anatomy. Once you know anatomy, you need to study physiology. Once you know anatomy AND physiology, you practice "being a doctor" by diagnosing what's wrong with real patients and devising strategies to solve their health problems. Once your training is over, now you are thrust into the "real world" where experience becomes your teacher.

The ultimate goal of studying how communication works is to solve "real world" relationship problems by improving your communication. These next lessons will be like your internship at the hospital.

You understand the anatomy of each relationship category from studying *How Relationships Work.* You've learned the "physiology" of communication by reading this book. Each one-way message has 6-steps that track the path of a message from Sender to a Receiver. Now, let's apply all these foundational principles to improve and/or monitor your personal "real world" relationships.

## I'm In A Problem Relationship, What Should I Do?

To truly tackle a "real world" relationship problem you ideally need both Copartners working together to solve it. But let's assume for the moment that you are the only person willing to evaluate and diagnose this problem relationship. It's gradually dawned on you that an important relationship is not working as expected. What is your strategy to problem-solve this difficult situation?

First you think about and parse as many factors as possible so that you have it all straight inside your head. This starts with the anatomy of your relationship. Use Part II of *How Relationships Work* to investigate and evaluate the Environment, Structure, and Two-Copartners of your relationship. In Part III, pick the relationship under consideration and run through all the questions to evaluate your current situation. I predict that 80% of the time this alone will reveal the cause of your problem.

If all the anatomical parts of your relationship check out and appear to be functional, you now know that excellent communication will be needed to address your problem. If you are a bit nervous about speaking with your Copartner directly, you might wish to review the situation with a friend or therapist using the metaphors in this book to describe your situation. Their feedback should be very helpful in this regard.

If you have a strong bond with your Copartner, then ideally it will be easy enough to schedule some "talk time" and go over the situation based on your understanding. The first few times you begin conversing on this level of honesty, it may be difficult. There could be a lot of "sharing" involved.

The more you do this, the more you will learn. Eventually, as you gain confidence with these ideas and your ability to communicate them, you will be able to diagnose problems quickly and take immediate steps from your side to resolve them. Eventually your skills will become second nature.

As you consider each factor of a problem relationship, you'll soon realize what is wrong or out of balance. When it's something on your side, then you can correct it, thus allowing your relationship to improve. If your personal assessment is that your Copartner is the major factor, then you know to discuss it with your him/her. Ideally, they will welcome your communication, but this is not always the case.

## Communicating About Your Relationships

Some people find it difficult to initiate problem-solving in their relationships for a variety of reasons. First, they may not be fully aware of their true thoughts and feelings. They may have strong thoughts and/or feelings but be unaware of which side of their inner conversations (between their Inner Child and Inner Parent) is making the case. This is further complicated by the idea that either side could voice a similar sounding argument, based on the circumstances.

If you aren't clear about what's happening inside your mind, you can be reluctant to discuss it on the outside. This is where practicing the SELF-Parenting Program is one way to get a good handle on both sides of what your inner voices are saying, especially concerning outer relationships.

This brings up the reminder that each person is 100% responsible for their 50% side of the seesaw. It's vital that you a strong grasp of your self-talk before you engage with your Copartner. Your mental thoughts and your emotional feelings can have conflicting opinions. One easy way to spot this situation is summed up by the following statement:

"One part of me wants ___________________
and
the other part of me wants ___________________

And, it turns out that these two options are completely incompatible. This would be an example of indecision and inner conflict on your side of the outer relationship seesaw. Your thoughts are saying one thing and your emotions are saying the opposite.

Secondly, assuming you are aware of your concerns in the form of unmet needs, you may have difficulty expressing this verbally. Perhaps this correlates with prior experiences such as when you tried to communicate in the past, only matters just got worse anyway.

Perhaps you don't want to bring up problems so as to not rock the boat. What you have is better than nothing, so you don't want to lose even this. Obviously, these are not strong positions to begin solving a relationship problem.

Another potential difficulty can occur when you delay communicating about a problem for too long. Eventually you decide it's easier to give up on the relationship than deal with the difficulty of bringing up communication. In this situation, it is important to make your last stand while you still care about the relationship.

You might be amazed how easily what appears to be a major problem can be quickly resolved, if you just bring it up before the relationship becomes unsalvageable. What appears to be a major problem to you, might not even register with your Copartner. Your fears might be all on your side of the seesaw. Yet you could convince yourself to jump off your side of the relationship for a baseless self-inflicted reason.

Another advantage to discussing unresolved problems as soon as they present themselves is to avoid any future escalation of troubles as your relationship moves forward. Discussing sooner rather than later is best for everyone concerned. Not every relationship is forever. In fact, the only relationship lasting forever is the SELF-Parenting relationship between your Inner Parent and Inner Child.

Another factor is your childhood programming. Your parents and early childhood trained your ability and skill set for solving relationship/communication problems by watching, learning, and acting how they solved their relationship problems (including with you). This formed the foundation for your current problem-solving patterns.

Since so few members of society are specifically taught positive communication skills, it's entirely possible that your parents never had the advantage that you have. They too had to learn by attending the school of hard knocks without the benefit of reading this book.

The patterns you were taught and learned to resolve in your family problems became your current template for the way you apply them to problem-solving as an adult. Becoming aware of these patterns is crucial yet it can also be difficult. These instructions are deeply set within your operating system. Here is another area where the SELF-Parenting Program shines, as a way of bringing insight to any internal problem-solving issues.

It's also possible that you are completely in touch with your thoughts and feelings and don't need SELF-Parenting at all. Yet your Copartner may be in the dark from his/her side of the seesaw. Many factors can contribute to a relationship that is not working ideally.

Your mission is to apply what you've learned to the best of your ability. Begin to communicate consciously with your problem Copartner in a personal relationship. The more you practice the better you'll get. Conscious communication gives any problem situation your best chance for a positive outcome.

The rest of this chapter offers clues and techniques, but it is "in your doing" that you will learn the importance of this material. The basic premise is to inundate you with a variety of topics and to provide questions you can ask yourself and/or your Copartner about your relationship.

These areas are designed to motivate you to initiate and facilitate relationship communication. These questions give you the raw knowledge you need to apply the concepts of *How Communication Works* to a "real world" laboratory — your life.

Based on what you've learned so far, let's review the following factors:

- What is the first key to communicating in a relationship?
- What is the second key to communicating in a relationship?
- What is the third key to communicating in a relationship?

Part of this puzzle involves whether you are the Sender or the Receiver. For this next section, take your role as the Sender.

## What Is the First Key to Communicating in A Relationship?

Always pay attention to your Inner Conversations. Your Inner Conversations are the key to your needs. Inside your mind you have two voices, your Inner Parent and Inner Child. These voices represent your thoughts and your feelings. Your two inner selves constantly discuss what each self wants and needs back and forth on an ongoing basis. They can even argue and disagree.

The more you pay conscious attention to your Inner Conversations, the sooner you will know what your Personal (Physical, Emotional, Mental) and Relational (Family, Social, Work) needs might be. For example, your mind might want one solution from a relationship and your emotional self might want another.

Having a clear idea of what your needs are before attempting to translate them into words and actions, is the easiest way to avoid communication problems, at least from your side of the GAP. Other terms that people use to represent this inner conversation is their self-talk, their intuition, or listening to "their gut" which is giving them a strong perspective on how they feel.

If you begin with your deepest thoughts and feelings, you have your best chance for a successful outcome. If you are motivated by some external standard or social perception, you are further away from your own Life-Space.

Use the keywords of physical, emotional, and mental to clarify which type of need you have. Review the need categories in *How Relationships Work* for both roles in your problem relationship. It's vital to be able to specifically name the precise need you want the relationship to meet.

Keep in mind that you are only half of a relationships seesaw. Your Copartner is the other half. S/he may or may not be in touch with his/her Inner Conversations. This is part of the fun. But do your best to know what your needs are from your side of the relationship. Let your Copartner worry about his/her half of the relationship seesaw.

## What Is the Second Key to Communicating in A Relationship?

Always strive to translate your thoughts and feelings (unmet needs) into words and actions that are Third-Party verifiable. Writing them out can be helpful. You can practice in front of a mirror or even tape yourself. This way you will know, at least from your side, that what you are striving to communicate is clear. This is easier said than done but doesn't have to be too difficult. If you know and are being honest about your needs, then it's actually quite easy. Just as with learning any new skill, the more you practice the better you'll get.

## What Is the Third Key to Communicating in A Relationship?

Even when you do an excellent job of knowing your needs and accurately translate them into observable behavior, keep your attention on the Receiver to assess if s/he appears to be interpreting your OB properly. If not, your communication may still be unsuccessful.

You can keep a watchful eye on both sides of your relationship seesaw but in truth, you only have jurisdiction and responsibility for your half. If the other person doesn't do right on his/her side, your relationship is doomed no matter how wonderful you may be or act.

## Every Communication Problem Has One Of Two Causes:

To make things ultra-simple, there are only two possible problems in the basic pattern of communication:

- The Sender is doing a poor job of translating his or her thoughts and feelings into observable behavior.

or

- The Receiver is incorrectly interpreting the observable behavior of the Sender.

There is a difference between a relationship problem and a communication problem. It may be that neither side likes what is being communicated. But if the interaction is clear and understood by both Copartners, this is preferable to any misunderstanding between them. If the communication is clearly understood, that is good. If neither side likes what the other is honestly communicating, this is a different, it's a problem with the relationship.

**Define Your Problem**

What is the exact problem that you want to solve? For this you need to define it. One way to do this is to:

- Write a clear description of the Copartner behavior or relationship issue that is creating the problem from your side.
- Figure out which Copartner is upset by the behavior, and thus owns the problem.
- Communicate with your Copartner about the problem and see if a win/win resolution can be achieved.

**Here Are Some Examples:**

Family:

- Child is banging on a pot making noise; Parent is unhappy.
- Sibling 1 is singing really loud; Sibling 2 can't read her book.
- Adult Child wants his/her Aging Parent to baby sit; Aging Parent want to go to a social event.

Social:

- Friend A is waiting for Friend B who never shows up; Friend A upset. Friend B is not concerned at all.
- Boyfriend is dating more than one Girlfriend; Girlfriend is unhappy. (Or vice versa.)
- Neighbor A is mowing the lawn at 5 am; Neighbor B next door is upset from the noise.

Work:

- The Boss is never around; The Employee has no direction.
- Coworker A leaves a messy workplace; Coworker B on the next shift has extra work to clean up before s/he can start work.
- A Coworker wants to meet outside work as "friends;" you don't. (Or vice versa.)

## How Communication Problems Are Solved

You begin solving relationship problems when you begin communicating. If you have a problem with a Copartner and are not communicating, then this problem has zero chance of truly going away.

If you are the one with the problem, you want to make sure it is a problem with the outer relationship and not a conflict between you and your Inner Child. If your problem specifically involves meeting a need provided by the other side of the relationship then yes, you do need to initiate dialog with your Copartner for your need to be met.

If your Copartner has the problem, then it is up to you to be a good Receiver on your side and help your Copartner resolve his/her issue. If your Copartner doesn't want to deal with their issue or concern, there's not much you can do.

## Problem Ownership: Who Owns the Problem

Problem ownership is a key concept that affects relationships in many ways. For example, which Role in the relationship owns the problem, provides the key as to how to solve it. There are many factors such as:

- Who has a need that is not being met? This is the person with the problem.
- What do you do when you own the problem?
- How do you get your own problem solved?
- How do you help a Copartner recognize a problem they cause but don't have; but you do?
- How do you help your Copartner solve a problem they have; but you don't?

An excellent resource for the "problem ownership" situation is discussed in books such as *Parent Effectiveness Training,* or *Leadership Effectiveness Training,* by Thomas Gordon. His descriptions are excellent and where I learned much of what I know about solving communication issues.

Have a clear idea of what you want to communicate before bringing up a problem with your Copartner. If you understand how the relationship is designed to work, you will have a realistic expectation of what this relationship provides and how to proceed.

You can ask yourself many questions to clarify your mind before sharing your thoughts and feelings across the GAP in a TPV manner. Sorting out these questions in advance will help you in many ways. The following questions can help you gather and distill your thoughts and feelings concerning a problem relationship.

Notice that the answers to ALL these questions involve you, on your side of the seesaw. Having a conscious answer to each question will help define your needs. You'll be able to sort out exactly how you feel, before discussing any issues with your Copartner. You might even find that answering these questions to your own satisfaction "solves" your relationship problem in one form of another.

### Clarifying Your Thoughts About This Relationship

- What relationship seesaw are you in with this person? Is it the correct one?
- Is this person on the seesaw with you? Is your Copartner truly on the other side?
- Is there a possibility that your Copartner feels s/he is on another type of relationship seesaw and not on the seesaw you believe?
- Would you each agree you are playing the correct role in this relationship?
- Do you know and understand the generic principles of the exact relationship seesaw you are on?

- Are any environmental aspects of the relationship affecting you negatively?
- What expectations do you have about this relationship that are not being met?
- What is your objective evaluation of the positive potential of this relationship?
- What is your objective evaluation of the negative potential of this relationship?
- Are your needs more personal inside your mind, or do they require an outer relationship?
- What physical needs are you trying to meet?
- What emotional needs are you trying to meet?
- What mental needs are you trying to meet?
- What relational needs are you trying to meet?
- How does this relationship provide the potential to supply these needs?
- Is your relationship currently meeting these needs for you? If so, why are you doing this evaluation?
- Were your needs met in this relationship until recently and now they are not?
- Have some specific needs never been met, and you are just now realizing this for the first time?
- How well have you defined your specific needs and how clearly do they fit into the relationship structure you are on?

## Interpreting Your Copartner's Third-Party Verifiable Behavior

**These factors involve the OB of your Copartner:**

- Is your Copartner doing anything within your relationship that you are unhappy with? This refers to anything specific to your interactions.
- Is your Copartner doing anything outside your relationship that you are unhappy with?
- What TPV behavior are you most unhappy with?
- What has been your prior response to your Copartner's TPV behavior?
- What changes do you feel might be more appropriate?
- Does your Copartner do positive things in your relationship that you are happy with?
- What TPV behavior are you most happy with?
- What TPV behavior are you not happy with?
- Has something changed about your Copartner recently that is bothering you?
- Does your Copartner know what TPV behavior is?
- What does your Copartner do to contribute to the goals of your relationship that is TPV?
    - According to you?
    - According to your Copartner?
- What does your Copartner NOT do to contribute to the goals of your relationship that is TPV?
- How would you like your Copartner to act so s/he contributes more to meeting your needs?

**Your Behavior**

- Do you fully understand what TPV behavior is?
- What are you doing to contribute to the goals of your relationship that is TPV?
    - According to you?
    - According to your Copartner?
- What are you not doing to contribute to the goals of your relationship?
    - According to you?
    - According to your Copartner?
- What would your Copartner like you to do to contribute to meeting his/her needs?
- What does your Copartner say is wrong with you or your behavior in the relationship?

**Questions You Can Ask Yourself:**

- Does my Copartner?
    - Spend time with me?
    - Make personal sacrifices on my behalf?
    - Act in a consistent manner?
    - Share his/her thoughts and feelings?
    - Act like s/he likes me?
    - Fill your cup, i.e. meet your needs?
- Do I enjoy being with my Copartner?

**What Specific Things Do I Do to Make My Copartner Happy?**

List some specifics:

- I load/unload the dishwasher.
- I vacuum.
- I do the grunt work.

- I do my writing.
- I work overtime.
- I gave them a ride.
- I loaned them money.
- I drove him/her to _______ for _______.

Whatever you believe you do for this person that is part of the relationship's structure should go here.

### Your Copartner's Positive HRW Traits for You?

Do any of your problems with you or your Copartner revolve around these trait issues? On a scale of 1-10, for the following traits, my Copartner:

- Is Attracted to me ___________
- Is Committed to me ___________
- Is Genuine with me ___________
- Is Trustworthy with me ___________
- Is Emotionally Mature ___________
- Has Communication Skills ___________
- Has Problem-Solving Skills ___________

### Do I Have Positive HRW Traits for My Copartner?

For my Copartner on a scale of 1-10, I:

- Am Attracted ___________
- Am Committed ___________
- Am Genuine ___________
- Am Trustworthy ___________
- Am Emotionally Mature ___________
- Have Communication Skills ___________
- Have Problem-Solving Skills ___________

The answers to the above questions will tell you if you, or possibly your Copartner, has made a bad choice for a Copartner. Once you have sorted through these questions, you will know and understand the traits issues that trouble you. They will help you to clearly begin the problem-solving process. If you have a problem with your Copartners traits, this is very difficult to overcome with communication.

This is a good time to remind you that there is no magic formula for one person to solve a two-person problem. There is no guarantee you will be successful at solving a true relationship problem by yourself, no matter how hard you try or how well you communicate from your side.

It is very comforting to know what is wrong from your perspective. At least on your side of the seesaw you can be clear. Using the prior questions, you will have an accurate and detailed understanding of the exact area troubling your relationship. Is it the environment? Is it that you don't think your Copartner is on the seesaw? Is it that his/her tactics are making you ill?

Another way to get at the raw material behind your problem is to write out your Inner Conversations about the relationship. If something is wrong enough that you are contemplating discussing it with your Copartner, you will be having a constant inner conversation going on about it inside your mind.

By writing out your inner conversations about the relationship, you'll get to the bottom-line issues bothering you. And this bottom line is going to be:

- An unmet need.
- Something you are not getting from the relationship that you expect or deserve.
- Something you "are getting" from the relationship that you do not like or deserve.
- Something about the Environment.
- Something about the Relationship Seesaw.
- Something about your Copartners traits or tactics.

**The next question is:**

Is this "something" the relationship structure promises to provide? If the answer is yes, then this is where you start. It's time to strategize your plan.

# {Ch 13} Strategizing Your Plan

This chapter contains more ideas designed to motivate you to solve a difficult relationship.

## Create a TPV Record of the Problem

If there is something your Copartner is doing that bothers you, then it's nice to have TPV evidence before you begin communicating. Writing down what you think is wrong is one way to create a TPV record for this purpose.

Simply write down on 3 x 5 cards the TPV behavior that your Copartner is doing that you don't like. Start with a heading that lists the exact problem you have. Under this heading, write out the needs you are looking to meet in terms of their physical, emotional, mental category. Or frame them as relationship needs this relationship is meant to provide. Do not specifically reference the other person's behavior. Some examples:

**Problem: my husband reads the papers with his shoes off and smells up the living room.**

- I have a physical need to be able to breathe freely in our living room.
- I have an emotional need to feel happy in my own home.
- I have a mental need to feel respected in our marriage.
- I have a social need to keep the house free of bad odors.

**Problem: My friend calls me to go out and then never shows up.**

- I have a physical need to spend my time appropriately.
- I have an emotional need to feel valued.
- I have a need for Friends that treat me with respect.
- I have a social need to spend my free time doing things I like with people who respect and like me.

Once you have written down the problem and named your needs, you are clear as to what you want to discuss. Now you can continue in a disciplined manner.

## Is Your Copartner in A Receptive State of Mind?

Before you can begin a potentially involved conversation with your Copartner, you need to make sure s/he has no undue pressures that will burden your discussion. The type of relationship seesaw you are on will determine a suitable time to bring up a relationship discussion.

Obviously, if it is a Family bond, the environment and timing for your discussion will be different than if your relationship has a Social or Work setting. In any case, you will want to check with your Copartner that this is an okay time for discussion.

You can do this by asking one of the following introductory questions such as:

- How was your day?
- How are things going at the moment?
- How are you feeling right now?
- Are you able to talk right now?
- Do you have some time to go over something?

Before asking, assess your Copartners current body language and emotional state. The key here is make fairly certain that you are asking at a good time. You don't want a rebuff from the get-go if you can easily anticipate and avoid it.

Even if you know it's probably a good time, ask the above questions anyway to test the waters. What you want to avoid here, is your Copartner giving you a "No" answer because s/he has some issue going on of which you are unaware. If there are no external circumstances and your Copartner is still reluctant to discuss your relationship, this becomes an escalation of the problem right there.

## Begin Your Discussion

Once your Copartner has agreed that s/he can speak with you, open your conversation with the following statement.

**I would like to discuss some aspects of our relationship.**

This statement is preparatory to introducing your discussion. You are letting your Copartner know the topic you want to discuss is about your relationship.

Ideally your Copartner will give you some sign of positive feedback to show s/he is willing to continue this conversation. If s/he starts in with a litany of complaints about you from your statement alone, you know you are in deep trouble.

If s/he is listening and seems agreeable to a discussion, all is well. Then you can make one of the following opening statements using your own words. You may want to write these down beforehand. Simply choose the statement that best fits your situation:

- I would like to discuss the Environment of our relationship.
- I would like to discuss the Roles in our relationship.
- I would like to discuss some of the Rules related to our relationship.
- I would like to discuss some Customs associated with our relationship.

- I would like to discuss some of your Traits as associated with our relationship.
- I would like to share some of my Needs with you in our relationship.
- I am not happy with some of the Tactics you are using in our relationship.

These are direct statements based on your understanding of how relationships work. They may be a bit strong as opening statements, but they are suggested here so you can be clear about the relationship area you want to discuss.

Ideally, you'll approach this discussion with a "soft introduction" especially if the relationship is new or you haven't discussed relationship issues before. As stated previously, your best results will come when both Copartners have read *How Relationships Work* and are familiar with the basic principles. However, this is unlikely if it is a new relationship.

Once the conversation has begun, be prepared to go where the discussion leads you. You are going to take this opportunity to explain what is bothering you about the relationship. You will have clear discussion points readily at hand from your prior preparation.

**Items to Discuss:**

- Assess the Environment of your relationship including the positive and negative influences.
- Discuss your respective relationship roles and what they mean to each Copartner.

- Discuss any relevant factors of your relationship structure.
- Explore and agree on the generic rules that apply to your relationship.
- Discuss the consequences of breaking the rules.
- Pay attention to if your/their rules match the generic standards.
- Discuss the customs that might apply to your ethnic, political, social, or religious backgrounds.
- Discuss the importance and evaluation of traits.
- Discuss your needs and those of your Copartner.

The more prepared you are from your side about your needs and what you want, the more relaxed you can be. This preparation also helps you to use positive tactics such as monitoring the emotional/mental state of your Copartner. Things may go well with both of you cooperating fully. But you also want to be careful to watch for possible adverse reactions.

You may have to spend a lot of time listening to an upset Copartner. You may need to stand up for your side if your Copartner likes to bully people. Some Copartners perceive communication about a relationship as an attack or threat rather than a helpful tactic. This is one reason writing down your thoughts and needs in advance is so valuable.

If your relationship issue specifically concerns your Copartner's traits, this can be a sensitive area of discussion. It also may reveal that your Copartner may not be as wonderful as you may have assumed or hoped for in the beginning. The possibility of hurt feelings or counter-attacks may be present.

During this whole time there will be a high stakes Sender/Receiver dynamic taking place. It may be hard for you to stay conscious of the 6-steps of communication as they occur "live and in person." Just do your best. The more you practice communication skills the more skilled you will become until it just becomes part of who you are.

## Questions You Can Ask Your Copartner

You would like to know your Copartner's thoughts and feelings. Clearly the setting and background of your relationship (F,S,W) will determine the emotional feeling, mood, or timing in which you present these questions assuming you even have this option.

Given your situation, here are sample questions you can frame within the context of your relationship roles and hope you get honest answers:

- Is this relationship a priority for you?
- Are you happy in this relationship?
- Would you like to invest more time and energy (or end) this relationship?
- Do I fill your cup?
- Do I make you happy in this relationship?
- What was your intended effect when you ________________________? (Describe OB)
- Do you have or feel any external restraints or pressures?
- Do you have any problems with your/my religious beliefs?

- Do. you have any issues with my/your moral beliefs, background, education, status, gender?
- Are there any complications involving your/my Family/Social/Work pressures?
- Do you have any other priorities or obligations that affect or conflict with our relationship?

## Communicating Your Needs

A primary cause of relationship conflict is that people don't know how to communicate their needs in a TPV way. Your ultimate goal is to communicate your unmet needs and ask your Copartner to meet them in the nicest way possible.

You have already determined in advance:

- What your relationship structure is, and the roles involved.
- That your relationship structure is meant to meet the need you have.
- The exact nature of your specific need and how you don't feel it is being met.

This means that you are willing and prepared to present your relationship expectations directly to your Copartner. This is strong stuff. You are calling out your Copartner because it is his/her role to meet your need as it is your role to meet theirs. If you are playing fair like you are supposed to, it is only fair that your Copartner reciprocate.

## If You Have A Problem in A Relationship, How Do You Fix It?

Two steps help you solve relationship problems: First, define your need to determine if you are to fulfill it internally or externally.

Is your need physical, emotional, or mental? If so, it may not involve the other person.

Does your need involve the other person? If so how, and what aspect of their role would meet this need?

## What Is an Internally Fulfilled Need?

An internally fulfilled need is one that involves your personal physical, emotional, or mental health. It involves your body, emotions, and/or mind. You fulfill these needs best by cooperating between your Inner Parent and Inner Child "on the inside." Another person or relationship is not meant to be involved.

For example, low self-esteem is not a need that is supposed to be fulfilled by another person. If someone else knows you and believes you are perfect, this is wonderful. They may tell you all day how pleasing and magnificent you are which is nice. However, if you lose this person in your life for some unrelated reason, you could possibly go into a deep depression because you no longer feel the external self-esteem this relationship gave you.

In which case you didn't really have self-esteem in the first place. You had what could be called, "outer-esteem" or "social esteem." If you don't feel self-esteem on your own within your Inner Conversations, you can have

10,000 people singing your praises from dusk till dawn and it won't help when you are alone.

History is littered with famous people who had the praise of everyone around them (plus all the money in the world) but were too damaged on the inside for outer praise to override their inner criticism and lack of self-esteem.

If your need is truly physical, emotional, or mental then it's meant to be fulfilled internally. Dialog between your Inner Parent and Inner Child within your Inner Conversations will identify and clarify these needs.

Daily SELF-Parenting sessions over time are the best way to clarify the various needs between your Inner Parent and Inner Child. What you learn from this practice is ongoing, cumulative, and increases in depth and understanding over time.

## What Is an Externally Fulfilled Need?

An externally fulfilled need is one that requires an outer relationship, i.e. Family, Social, or Work, or possibly Professional. Your need is fulfilled by the person on the other side of the relationship. No other way will work. There is no amount of positive SELF-Parenting that can fulfill an outer need other than giving up your desire for this need to be met.

These types of needs also involve PEM needs. They just happen to be physically, emotionally, or mentally provided by your Copartner as a part of their role. Let's discuss some simple examples.

A person has a physical need to eat. But it's the role of the Parent/Child Relationship that the Parent physically feed the Child. The Parent meets a physical need of the Child.

Every person has a need to be support him/herself emotionally, but one of the roles of a Sibling would be to support her/his Sibling emotionally. This might take the form of support where a Sibling encourages his/her sibling to achieve some goal such as becoming a cheerleader, learning to ride a bike, or applying for a job.

Each person has a level of mental curiosity, but another person could challenge and motivate them to learn an entirely new skill. Neighbor A could inspire Neighbor B to learn the physical and mental skills to become a car mechanic. Neighbor B was motivated to learn through Neighbor A's example and support.

## Relational Needs:

Some needs can only be provided by the relationship. Unless you have a relationship of the right kind the need cannot be met. For example, you may be expected to bring your spouse to a wedding. If you don't have a spouse, or he/she won't go, no other person could take their place. It's only the Social Copartner from this relationship that can fulfill the social need.

We call these Relational Needs and they can be quite important, especially in some cultural and political circumstances. If your need must be externally fulfilled, to solve your problem you must:

- Understand its PEM obligation.
- Define how the outer relationship meets your need.
- Communicate your need to your Copartner.
- Ask that this need be fulfilled.

If your need is NOT one your relationship Copartner can fulfill, this may require you to seek a new relationship structure, or possibly a professional relationship.

## Problem Ownership: Who Owns the Problem? Who Has the Unfulfilled Need?

When solving a relationship problem, clarifying which Copartner has the problem is essential. Three choices are available:

- You have the problem (unmet need) on your side of the seesaw.
- Your Copartner has the problem (unmet need) on his/her side of the seesaw.
- You both have a problem. (Needs that are unmet for both Copartners or needs that are in direct conflict)

### What Are Some Ways to Meet Your Needs in A Relationship?

- Meet them yourself. (If you can meet this need yourself, then the relationship doesn't have to.)
- Have your Copartner meet them.
- Meet the need outside your relationship with the agreement of your Copartner.
- Change your desire for the need to be met.

### If Your Copartner Has A Denial Problem, How Can You Help Him/Her?

The denial of a relationship problem by your Copartner can be a difficult problem to overcome. The person in denial clearly has a personal fear or distress taking precedence over the health of your relationship. Invite her/him to share any thoughts and feelings. Listen for the unmet need and help them define and clarify what it might be. Next, see what you can do to help them fulfill this need. If your Copartner is in denial or oblivious to an unmet need, it's virtually impossible for them to resolve it on their own.

### You Both Have a Problem with Unmet Needs

The balanced exchange of energy by both Copartners is implied for a relationship to be successful. Meeting the other person's needs is your contribution towards this goal. Your Copartner should not be asked to meet his/her relational needs on their own; that is your job. Otherwise, why are you in this relationship in the first place?

If the other person is not expending energy on his/her side to meet your needs, then you have to be concerned about this as well. Hopefully by now, you are getting a sense of what this all means. Following is a comprehensive list of questions, topics and principles that can hopefully provide answers you are looking for.

## If You Have A Bad Relationship What Is Going Wrong?

On a more detailed level, you will find that there is a problem with the Environment, the Structure, the Two-Copartners or a combination of these three variables. Each type of relationship meets a generic set of unfulfilled needs. If your relationship is designed to meet a specific set of needs, and those needs remain unmet, you have a problem.

As you have seen, problems in relationships have a variety of causes. However, there are only three primary areas to start looking. Once you know where to look, finding the unmet need is much easier. What are the three areas? They are:

- The Environment
- The Seesaw Structure
- The Two-Copartners

Once identified your problem area can be solved, meaning your needs can be met and you will be happy. If your problem is not solved (your need is not being met), you will remain unhappy. Hopefully, even if difficult, you will remain motivated to seek the source of a problem.

Next are a series of questions that will give you clues to deep problems in a relationship. Depending on your exact set of circumstances, you may designate the problem as major or minor.

**Do You Have A Major Problem? This Relationship Does Not Exist.**

- One Copartner (or both) is not on the seesaw.
- One Copartner (or both) has bad traits.
- One Copartner (or both) is on a different relationship structure (equates to not being on the same seesaw.)
- One Copartner (or both) is not following their primary relationship role.

**Is This A Minor Problem? Your Relationship Is in Danger but Salvageable.**

- One Copartner has problems communicating.
- One Copartner (or both) is not getting needs met (temporary situation).
- One Copartner is using inappropriate tactics but is willing to reconsider.
- One Copartner has personal problems on his/her side of the GAP affecting their ability to function in his/her relationship role.
- One Copartner (or both) is following most, but breaking some relationship rules.

**Is There A Major-Major Problem? This Relationship Is Doomed.**

- Both Copartners have problems communicating.
- Both Copartners are using inappropriate tactics.
- Both Copartners are not getting needs met (permanent situation).

- Both Copartners have personal problems on their side of the GAP affecting their ability to function in the relationship.
- Both Copartners are breaking major relationship rules.

These problem areas as discussed above represent the deepest level of severe relationship issues.

If you have a current relationship that fits somewhere in the above list, you will be challenged to your utmost. Possibly the best use of these classifications is to see where and how your past failed relationships fit into these patterns and do your best to identify and prevent such future relationship problems before they devolve to this stage.

# {Ch 14} Suggested Communication Templates

Communicating unmet needs is the dirty chore of relationships, but someone has to do it. When you have unmet needs, it's your responsibility to communicate them. You may find, or your Copartner may point out, that the need you are asking for is not part of the generic needs met by your relationship. In this case, you must seek the relationship that meets this need or provide this need yourself within your Inner Parent and Inner Child relationship.

Relationships represent energy systems that occur as a result of the interplay between two fluctuating energy fields. Conflict is an obstacle to the smooth exchange of energy in a relationship. It blocks the flow of energy back and forth across the Mid-Gap Line.

Expect problems to develop in relationships from time to time. Even an excellent relationship can experience problems or even go bad. Conflict is the nature of reality. It's important to remain vigilant to potential relationship problems. Early warning signs must not be ignored. Keep in mind that you can't completely solve a relationship problem between Two-Copartners from only one side of the seesaw.

Most relationships of all types start out well during the honeymoon phase. This is the initial 2-3 months period where each Copartner is feeling optimistic and being on his/her best behavior. After around three months of ongoing interaction is when relationships begin to slide into the dysfunctional realm if unresolved conflicts start to accumulate.

Relationships are like gardens. If they are not maintained, they tend to get messy and turn to weeds. When both Copartners practice positive communication in a win/win way, then the relationship strengthens and becomes more secure over time.

In the "real world" most relationship problems are dealt with and resolved during the interactions of daily life between the Two-Copartners. In the main we can celebrate that humankind has many people from all cultures and walks of life who are exceptionally worthy as Copartners in their life relationships.

Ask yourself; what percentage of your current relationships are going well? If it's 80% or better, your relationships are in good shape. You might not even be putting that much conscious energy into them. Your life just hums along smoothly as expected. If your percentage is under 50% then perhaps it's time for you to start culling your negative relationships.

Not talking about a problem only makes matters worse. Both Copartners must be willing to discuss and work out various problems. However, it may be that the true problem exists outside of the relationship structure itself.

For example, one student of SELF-Parenting had a two-week Inner Conflict about a relationship that essentially turned out to be a "lack of money" problem. If s/he had the money, the relationship problem would not have existed at all. These things are not easy to see sometimes. S/he had a personal financial problem but was treating it as if it were a relationship problem, which it wasn't.

## Communication Template Suggestions

Following are some "templates" that provide questions you can use in various situations. Templates are simply a set of pre-planned questions that guide you towards dialog about a topic, in this case your relationship. It's up to you to pick and choose the ones that might be appropriate to your given circumstances. You can experiment with them based on your own context.

These questions provide a direct intro into a discussion when you are unhappy with a relationship.

- Ask your Copartner, "Are you happy with our relationship?"
- After they answer you can say, "I'm not."
- When they ask, "Why?" say, "Because my needs are not being met."
- When they ask, "What needs are those?" then tell them.

This next section provides a set of sentences to investigate deeper areas to ask about when you are unhappy with a relationship. Use them as they apply.

**Some Dialogue Sentences You May Find Useful:**

- "My needs are not being met in our relationship."
- "I am meeting your needs, but you are not meeting mine."
- "I have met your need in our (___________) relationship by _________, now I would like you to meet mine by _____________."
- "Just because you are experiencing a Win in our relationship doesn't mean that I'm happy."
- "I am wondering if our _________ relationship is dysfunctional. You may be happy and winning, but I don't feel like I am."
- "I believe that our relationship is not positive because I am experiencing a Lose in our relationship due to _____________."

**Communication Rules of Generic Human Relationships**

This section contains three rules that are useful to keep relationship conversations flowing.

- You must answer a direct question.
- You may not answer a question with another question.
- No answer is a "no" answer.

Be actively engaged and involved in your relationships. Relationships deteriorate with non-involvement by the Copartners.

## Questions to Ask Your Copartner:

Here are some open-ended questions that allow your Copartner to give you feedback. They are not confrontational and could be asked at any stage of a relationship.

- What is your current level of happiness with our relationship?
- Is there anything I can do to make our relationship better for you?
- On a scale of 1-10, how happy are you with our ________/_______ relationship?
    - Physically?
    - Emotionally?
    - Mentally?
    - Socially?
- Are you unhappy about anything with our ________/_______ relationship?
- Do you feel our relationship is mutually supportive/beneficial?
- Do you feel like our relationship is going well?
- Do you feel we have conflicting or competing interests?
- Is there anything you'd like to tell me about our relationship?
- Do you view our relationship as a win/win?

## Questions to Ask Yourself About "Ascribing" In a Relationship

If a person is continually trying to tell you how or what to think and feel, they have little respect for you as a person. Called "ascribing" as discussed earlier, this is a major barrier to relationship communication. This person is not willing to remain on his/her side of the seesaw or let you manage your side the way you see fit.

- Is ________ always trying to tell me what to think and feel?
- Does ________ stay on his/her side of the see-saw?
- Am I allowed to say what I think/feel and am I still accepted if I do?
- Is there a "my way or the highway" attitude from my Copartner?
- Can I communicate my thoughts and feelings fully without being interrupted or accused?
- Do ________ and I share equal conversation time?
- Does my Copartner ask me hinting, accusatory, or unpleasant questions?
- Am I told "what I feel or "why I do things"?
- Am I accused of thoughts, feelings, or motiva-tions I don't have?
- Does ________ ever automatically assume they know what I'm experiencing? And then act based on this like it's true?

## Self-Inquiry to End A "Problem Relationship"

When is it time to end a problem relationship? If your ongoing need does not require another person, then it is more of a Personal need. As explained, you pursue this type of need based on your SELF-Parenting relationship.

In this situation your communication is between your Inner Parent and Inner Child to figure out what steps you to take next. It will be either a physical, emotional, or mental action which you can easily access through SELF-Parenting exercises.

Does your need require another person? If so, what is the physical, emotional, or mental behavior by your Co-partner that will meet this need? What if your need is one that your relationship should fulfill, but is not? It may be that you have to end the relationship. To prepare for this you have already determined in advance:

- The relationship seesaw you are on including your role.
- How your relationship structure is meant to meet your need.
- What your need is and how it is not being met.
- That you have previously communicated your need to your Copartner in a TPV way?
- If this a new issue or if it has become more long-standing?
- How willing you are to continue with a losing relationship?

It is your Copartner's role to meet your need in the same manner as it is for you to meet theirs. If you are doing what you are supposed to do, it is only fair that your Copartner reciprocate.

Let's say you have made multiple genuine communications with your Copartner to the best of your ability on your side of the seesaw and nothing is forthcoming. In this situation you need a new Copartner or another relationship structure.

## Conclusion

People experience conflict in relationships because they cannot communicate their needs in a Third-Party Verifiable way. You have learned how to communicate your needs in as TPV way as possible. You understand that the ultimate purpose of communication is to clearly state your needs and ask your Copartner to meet them.

This book has provided a multitude of tools and scenarios that will enable you to diagnose, define, and repair practically any communication problem that can be repaired. If not, you will know why, and you will also have learned valuable life lessons as to what to watch out for as you engage in future relationships with new Copartners.

I wish you the best implementing these guidelines and using these tools. If you experience any problems that don't seem to be covered in this book, you are welcome to email me at:

dr_john_pollard@howrelationshipswork.com

# About the Author

Dr. John Pollard is a lifelong student and educator whose professional life defines the term holistic healer. Throughout his career, he has healed several thousands of individuals with diverse Body, Mind, and Relationship problems by means of the innovative system he originated, called Generic Human Studies (see book *What is Generic Human Studies?)*

He is the creator of the psychological system called SELF-Parenting which became known in the psychology profession as "inner child work" during the late 80s. (See book *SELF-Parenting: The Complete Guide to Your Inner Conversations.)*

His book *How Relationships Work* (HRW) introduced a completely original, extremely simple, yet supremely accurate explanation of how each of the 12 generic human relationships function in the "real world."

As an expert in digestive problems Dr. Pollard shares simple yet effective healing prescriptions in *The Digestive Awareness Diet*, which he used to heal a multitude of medical diagnostic failures over a 30-year career.

www.ingramcontent.com/pod-product-compliance
Ingram Content Group UK Ltd.
Pitfield, Milton Keynes, MK11 3LW, UK
UKHW020133250726
13967UKWH00002B/628